Dreams: Guide To The Soul

40 Ancient Secret Keys to Healing, Renewal and Power

By Steven Fox, Ph.D.

Edited by Lynn Shahan

Cover Art by Elisha Dorado

All images are licensed
from Shutterstock.com

Biographical details have been changed to protect the dreamers who are anonymous. No part of this book is intended as psychological, psychiatric or medical treatment or advice. Readers are urged to consult with experienced professionals for treatment of medical, psychiatric or psychological conditions.

Endorsements

"A fascinating exploration of the mysteries in the playground of the unconscious. Dr. Fox's book has already helped me to help my clients understand themselves in a whole new way by diving into the deepest parts of themselves and to discover their own answers to the problems of their lives."

Dr. Carmen L. Lucia, Licensed Clinical Psychologist

"Shakespeare's Hamlet said 'to sleep, perchance to dream' and Mama Cass sang 'dream a little dream of me.' Steve Fox's new book would have made good reading for either of them. An extensive review of principles of dream interpretation gleaned from years of clinical practice. Recommended."

Martin Boxer, MD

"I bought this book on the advice of a friend and thought it would be an interesting read. What I didn't count on was the extensive experience and research of the author in trying to seek real life meaning from the dreams of countless clients over the past 20 or so years of his practice."

Virginia

"This brilliant little tome is a dream analysis and exploration gem. If you are interested in Jungian concepts, from archetypes to dreams, or dream analysis in general then you will love this book. It is the kind of work that bears reading and re-reading."

HRR

"I found this book while searching for a dream interpretation guide. This one offers compelling and practical advice for understanding your dreams. The author states that our subconscious creates dreams to motivate, inspire, guide, or warn us--complete with age-old metaphors and archetypes--and condenses all the information into a brain infomercial."

Author L.Z. Marie

Author Bio

Dr. Steven Fox, a private-practice licensed psychologist with over 25 years experience, says, "Having this book at the beginning of my practice would have reduced the amount of time it took me to get to where I am now by at least ten years."

It was while recovering from complications from an experimental treatment for MS (which was ultimately successful) that Fox had a recurring dream that facilitated his recovery and led to his fascination with dreams and their meanings. Fox and his wife Deborah Brogan, M.D., a board certified psychiatrist, currently share a private practice office in Mesa, Arizona.

DEDICATION &
ACKNOWLEDGEMENTS

To My Loving Wife Debby, the Girl of My Dreams

Acknowledgments to My Dream Team:

Dream Editor of Editors: Lynn Shahan

Dream Jungian Analyst: Darlene Demmer

Dream Physical Therapist: Diana Munger

Dream Neurologist: Timothy Vollmer, M.D.

Dream Reviewers: Allan Mosby and Casey Vail

Dream Muse: Lizette Donovan

If You Are Seeking Help...

No part of this book is intended for psychological or medical treatment. Consult an experienced professional for personal guidance or treatment of medical, psychiatric, and/or psychological conditions or issues.

Many biographical details of dreamers have been disguised to protect the identities of the dreamers.

TABLE OF CONTENTS

CHAPTER 9:
MAJOR SYMBOLS OF
TRANSFORMATION 58

CHAPTER 10:
THE SHADOW – THE SOURCE
OF CHANGE 63

CHAPTER 11:
CLEANING UP YOUR LIFE 70

CHAPTER 12:
ARCHETYPES 78

CHAPTER 13:
THE SHADOW ARCHETYPE 82

CHAPTER 14:
THE TRICKSTER ARCHETYPE 85

CHAPTER 25:
NOURISHMENT AND NURTURE 143

CHAPTER 26:
CLOTHING IS PSYCHOLOGICAL
BODY ARMOR IN DREAMS 149

Chapter 27:
Alcoholism 157

Chapter 28:
Drugs 162

CHAPTER 29:
THANKS FREUD

CHAPTER 30:
HEALING

Chapter 34:
Dream Incubation 207

Chapter 35:
Questions..213

Chapter 36:
Lucid Dreams 219

CHAPTER 37:
LIKE FROM ANOTHER
PLANET, MAN 223

CHAPTER 38:
THE DEVIL IS IN
THE DETAILS 225

CHAPTER 39:
DIFFERENT KINDS
OF DREAMS 228

Welcome!

Welcome! You have made a great choice in entering the realm of Dream Discovery. In this book we are going to look at what dreams mean, and show you how that knowledge can improve your life and the lives of your family and friends.

After you read this book, you will be able to relax more and your brain will be able to guide you towards personal healing, connecting the conscious and subconscious because you have insight into what your dreams mean. You will have the chance for more prosperity, better relationships and more happiness in your life. In fact, I credit my own understanding of dreams with helping me to heal from multiple sclerosis, and my dreams helped my growth and evolution to believe in higher purposes for my life and ultimately heal my soul.

You will feel better about your dreams after you read this book, and if you don't finish the book, you may miss out on important symbolism that will help you in the future. You will be better able to listen to other people explain their dreams, and everyone has them!

So let's get started...

Finding Your Unique Path With Dreams

How do you unlock personal power with dreams? Dreams point out how and why we are not being effective. Dreams often suggest courses of action. That is the whole point of dream incubation, a process of asking your dreams questions which is described in Chapter 34. That is the thrust of the Shadow Archetype which is the most frequent source of change. The whole idea of archetypes, which are fixed patterns of thought in the subconscious, is that if you can tie into your most pervasive archetype, it increases your personal power and effect upon the world exponentially.

The **Queen Archetype** is about almost nothing other than power. The **Heroic Masculine Archetype** is the epitome of the person deciding to use their abilities for good. The **Trickster Archetype** is all about manipulative power management in situations that are almost impossible. The **Willing Sacrifice Archetype** is about refusing to use your personal power.

Males in dreams are an evaluation as to how the person's power is either being used or blocked. Females in dreams represent emotional management and their effect upon the dreamer's functioning in the world. The **Wise Old Man Archetype** dispenses fatherly advice regarding the dreamer's course of action. An overriding voice in a dream is a direct and urgent demand that warns the dreamer of consequences.

Dreams are frequently personal power management with the emotional and logistical situation nicely summed up in an often strange condensation designed to grab our attention.

After years of work as a private-practice clinical psychologist, I have compiled a list of the 40 most common and key themes in dreams, along with explanations of their meanings and several examples of how to interpret them, using actual dreams with the identity of the dreamer kept anonymous. A random sampling of the numerous themes and symbols covered includes water, flying, pets, animals, colors, food, and numbers. I give each symbol or theme its own chapter.

Psychological terms that may be unfamiliar are explained briefly initially. These same terms are later discussed in depth, often with their own chapter. Novel and psychological terms are defined in the short selective glossary. Following the interpretation chapters, a bibliography and reference list for those interested in further reading is provided. **The reader is urged to make frequent use of the selective glossary at the very end of this book. You may benefit from reading the whole glossary after you read several chapters.**

This book, *Dreams: Guide To The Soul*, follows a certain structure. A key is presented that is useful in interpreting a dream. Each dream will contain more information than just the illustration of one key because of the complex and multi-faceted nature of significant dreams. The other elements of a particular dream often either forecast what the next key will discuss or refer back to a previous key and set of dreams.

As such, the process of this book is more spiral than it is linear. The keys are repeated within the interpretation of each dream. By the end of the book, the reader is likely to find that many of the keys of dream interpretation are ingrained in the reader's mind.

There are forty proposed keys. These are processes I have observed in hundreds, if not thousands, of dreams. These keys are not information that I feel is speculative. I believe the keys are sound guidelines that one can trust.

In graduate school, a specific and comprehensive method of interpreting dreams was never actually offered. Instead, examples were given so that the therapist went on a grand "fishing expedition" and hoped that the catch was verified by the client's reaction. One can interpret dreams this way, but there are problems with such a loose and mostly atheoretical approach.

The main problem is the amount of time it takes to interpret a dream with a "fishing expedition" method. Carl Jung's dream interpretation gives the therapist guidelines on how to interpret a dream. Following a systematic method allows the dream to be interpreted much faster. During a typical single private practice therapy session, I often interpret four and up to six dreams. The client gets a wealth of information that their own subconscious supplies.

I always felt that I did a reasonable job of interpreting dreams in the beginning but did not really feel good at it until I did it for ten years. After twenty years, I felt that I was truly delivering interpretations that focused on the client and were beyond common sense. Having this book would have reduced the amount of time it took me to get to where I am now by at least ten years.

To get started, let me introduce a dream with its interpretation. Do not expect to fully understand the interpretations until you are well into the book. *Dreams: Guide To The Soul* is the beginning of developing a systematic approach to interpreting dreams, wherein the reader begins to develop the wherewithal to begin meaningfully and successfully interpreting dreams.

PREVIEW DREAM: YOU CAN'T OPERATE A SPEED-BOAT AT HOME

A 60-year-old retired teacher dreamt that a beekeeper acquaintance put a speedboat in her swimming pool. The dreamer was there trying to corral some kids to go to school, but couldn't remember where her car was. She was scarfing down M & Ms during the entire dream.

Preview Dream Interpretation

Knowing the dreamer's gender and age, there are perhaps several basic things that can be said about the dreamer. She is likely to be a person who usually is in control of her instincts which is what the image of a beekeeper represents. The beekeeper in the dream is an action part of her psyche that extracts sweetness, honey, from wild instinct (the birds and the "bees"). Water is emotion. Swimming pools are domestic emotion or emotion close to home (swimming pools are manmade and close to home).

Boats are used to navigate emotions in dreams. That it is a speedboat means she is in a hurry. That she has a speedboat in her swimming pool is frustrating because there is not much that can be done with a speedboat in a swimming pool. Her trying to corral kids to go to school means that there are relatively new parts of herself that need to learn more. That she cannot find her car means that she does not presently know how to get to or where to find the means to learn what she is uncertain about needing to learn. M & Ms are the classic reinforcers that are being eaten addictively in the dream. She is trying to be satisfied with

her current domestic situation, but is prone to experience "sugar highs" rather than total satisfaction.

The dream is screaming that she is trying to extract all the sweetness she can from life, but is presently frustrated with not knowing how to get there, as the present domestic means are impractical and/or hasty. She wants emotionally satisfying experiences, but is perplexed with trying to find a practical means to achieve this. The suggestion is that she may be quantitatively trying to increase her emotional satisfaction, while the dream suggests she needs a practical method to engage upon a qualitative change in the way she navigates her emotions. The school kids suggest she is trying to learn new ways to achieve emotional satisfaction. This is a person who is emotionally transitioning. The problems are that the old ways of getting to where she wants to go are lost and the new ways presently seem impractical. She wants to learn more emotionally so that she has more emotionally satisfying experiences. Her doing the same old things now may produce a sugar high, which can be fun but may feel like it lacks substance. The M & Ms are not as good for you, in contrast to the more substantial and natural honey, which she dealt with well in the past.

Some possible suggestions based on the dream: (1) one solution may be to seek more emotional satisfaction outside of the home (HER SPEEDBOAT NEEDS AN OCEAN OR AT LEAST A LAKE TO TRAVEL UPON). She may need a more expanded venue beyond her home; (2) new emotional learning is being strongly encouraged because she needs qualitative emotional change. She has the experience but not the practical means to get to where she wants to go emotionally. This is difficult because she does not know exactly where she wants the journey to go. She appears to be organizing herself for new learning, which is necessary for emotional satisfaction. The emphasis in this dream is more on emotional and less upon factual information. The short moral of this dream: One cannot operate a speedboat at home.

The dreamer later validated the interpretation of this dream by saying it was "right on." The dream interpretation fit her circumstances accurately as a retired teacher who was adjusting to less going on in her life and who was straining to find a new direction. The above is a complex interpretation that would not have been possible without using many of the forty keys expounded upon in this book. If you really want to know what dreams reveal about your inner self, you have come to the right place.

What do dreams unlock? They unlock the inner parts of your psyche. Each character is a different part of your mind, with men tending more toward actions and women tending more toward emotions. Conflicts are being resolved or demonstrated through the interaction of the different players in the dream. The recurrent dramas of persecutor, victim, and rescuer reverberate through the ages and appear as predictable archetypes in the individual's dreams. The temptation is to interpret dreams interpersonally rather than intrapsychically; however, it is through the dreamer identifying with and owning the various characters in the dream that true insight emerges. The ownership is the hardest and most rewarding part of dream interpretation. We frequently do not like nor accept the various characters springing from our psyche, but we need to know who is there to get more than common sense from a dream. **We need to know which archetype holds the key to exponentially increasing the dreamer's power.**

A MIRACLE REVEALED IN A DREAM

When did my interest in interpreting dreams begin? First, a bit of background information is necessary. I was born when I was eighteen. I should say that was actually the year of my psychological birth, forty years ago when I entered college at the University of South Dakota, leading to my becoming a clinical psychologist licensed in Arizona. The pregnancy was a difficult eighteen long years spent on a farm with a large and dysfunctional family where children were raised to tend the farm. By stark contrast, in college, abstract ideas were discussed and people actually thought I had something to say. I toyed with mathematics, computers, economics and sociology, but always had an affinity for psychology. My development in utero on the farm faded into the dimness and was overwhelmed by the conception of the world as a very large place where I could find myself. I received a double major in psychology and sociology and was ready for more.

After doing a five month undergraduate psychology internship at Norton State Hospital for the Mentally Retarded in Kansas, I entered the graduate Clinical Psychology program at the University of Montana. In graduate school, I saw clients under supervision from the start, in addition to doing a multitude of assistantships where I could integrate what I learned in the classroom with experience in applied settings, which included a psychiatric ward, a group private practice, a halfway house, a group home for the mentally retarded, and a state prison. I traveled to Boston, where I did a summer assistantship at the West Roxbury, VA, doing therapy with paralyzed and brain injured veterans. I taught Introductory Psychology 101 during my fourth year in graduate school. While doing all this, I always saw four or five psychotherapy clients from the Missoula, Montana community at large per week throughout graduate school through the affiliated clinical psychology clinic. One of my practicums was at a different counseling clinic that focused upon university students. I started out being behavioral in orientation, added the cognitive perspective, absorbed humanistic psychology and increasingly drifted into psychoanalytic therapy. Both my Master's Thesis (Fox & Wollersheim, 1984) and my Doctoral Dissertation (Fox & Walters, 1986), as well as an experiment I did in independent study (Fox, Sturm & Walters, 1984), were published.

My fifth year of graduate school was spent doing an internship at a consortium in Albany, New York, which included a VA, a medical center hospital psychiatric ward, and an outpatient clinic in a state hospital. I had the good fortune of meeting my wife, Deborah Brogan, M.D., who was a fourth-year psychiatric resident at the time. We both attended a post-graduate outpatient psychotherapy study group, which was a retro Freudian group that followed the teachings of Dr. Robert Langs, who was the mentor for the group's leader, John Thibodeau, Ph.D.

I subsequently worked in a psychiatric ward of a medical hospital and then for New York State, screening correctional officers for the prisons, before marrying my wife. We both then worked in different divisions of a Community Mental Health Clinic in Albany, New York for over three years. During that time, Deborah became board certified as a psychiatrist in New York State and I became licensed in New York as a psychologist. I subsequently became a member of the *National Register of Health Service Providers in Psychology.* My wife indicated she needed far more sun than was willing to shine in Albany, so we moved to Phoenix, Arizona in 1988. I rented a small office and started private practice, which I have been doing since. My wife, Deborah Brogan, M.D., who worked for Arizona State University as a board certified psychiatrist, joined me in also doing some private practice in 1994. We currently share a private practice office in Mesa, Arizona.

The Author's Healing from Multiple Sclerosis (MS)

I was diagnosed with multiple sclerosis in January 1991. The first five years, it was not noticeable from the outside. I entered psychotherapy with a Jungian analyst who was trained in dream interpretation at Carl Jung's Institute in Zurich, Switzerland. I was amazed at the insights achieved through this form of therapy. More than that, I was struck by the fact that my dreams very often gave direct advice about how best to handle my illness and life. Carl Jung's methods reached deeper levels of myself. What looked like distorted nonsense in my dreams frequently turned out to be keen insights and a call to action.

Multiple Sclerosis (MS) is an autoimmune disorder in which the immune system attacks the insulation (the myelin) coating the fibers of the nervous system. This deconstruction of the nerve fibers leads to various electrical or nervous system problems with vision, walking, balance, strength, incontinence, vertigo, etc. The symptoms are dependent upon which nerve fibers or brain cells are being attacked.

I gradually and slowly deteriorated, until in 2005 I received a brace on my right leg. I was also using a cane. That did not prevent me from having one or two major falls per week.

I was headed for a wheelchair. I found a treatment on the Internet which involved having an infusion of a big bag of steroids each day for three days in a row. On the fourth day, I was given an infusion of cytoxan, a strong immune system suppressor. The theory was to kill off the part of the immune system attacking the neurons in my brain and spinal cord. The hope was that the regenerated immune system would be a kinder and gentler one that quit attacking the insulation of the brain and nervous system. The above treatment was given every three to six months for two years, and *voila!* It worked.

I ran into difficulties around 2005 because I was also taking betaseron at the time, in combination with the steroids and cytoxan. I gave myself an injection of betaseron every other day to prevent MS attacks. All the steroids, cytoxan and the betaseron had the effect of drastically lowering my immune system. I developed a severe infection in my left leg and had to be hospitalized.

While in the hospital, I had a dream that felt more like a vision. The dream was so intense and vivid that it almost seemed real. The **primal image** is seared into my memory to this day. I dreamt that Native American medicine men were dancing around me, shaking percussion instruments that sounded like hundreds of beads rhythmically hitting seashells all at once. They were nearly running as they danced around me with high kicks (I was a long distance runner in high school and was in karate shortly before the multiple sclerosis was diagnosed).

IMPLEMENTING THE DREAM VISION

I was released from the hospital after the infection was operated upon. The wound was left partially open because an infected wound should not be completely closed. I was given a PICC line in my arm, the infusion stand, and instructions on how to give myself three infusions of antibiotics per day. I continued doing my psychotherapy private practice and was also in physical therapy. The infection was severe to the point that I wore a machine on the wound that gently sucked debris and infection from the wound. I kept thinking about the intense dream or vision I had in the hospital. Vivid dream visions like that typically have much to teach if we pay attention. When the dreamer is ready, the right dream will appear.

I took the dream vision to mean that I needed to do physical activity. Specifically, the medicine men running and kicking in this **very archetypal dream** meant that I was supposed to engage in vigorous physical activity like I did in my long distance running and karate days. With guarded but determined belief, I decided to engage in vigorous physical therapy with new fervor. I worked out at a physical therapy facility that had parallel bars surrounding me while I exercised so I could catch myself when I fell at least twice per week.

The dream recommending running was a harder thing for me to consider. Run? It was all I could do to walk with a cane and a plastic brace that went from my right toes almost to my hip. I decided to ask my dreams and subconscious to send a sign to me in a dream when it was time for me to try running. The answer came about two months later.

I had built my stamina up somewhat with the help of the best physical therapist in the world, Diana Munger, who I had been seeing for about two years at that point. She had a practical doctorate in physical therapy and was a yoga instructor. She could glance at me, tell me what muscles were not working right, and then design exercises to remedy the situation. It was then that I had a curious dream. I dreamt that I did a flying full roundhouse Taekwondo kick, which takes considerable coordination. I decided that it was time to run.

With great trepidation, I made my way to the road that early fall morning. I started walking fast and then ventured a mild trot. I kept waiting for my ankles, knees or legs to twist, followed by my crashing to the gravel. I went for a block and started to relax after two and then three blocks. It was not pretty, and I did not set any speed records, but I was throwing one leg after the other into the air, followed by somewhat flat footed but adequate landing of each foot. Glory to God, I could run again.

Was it the medicine? Was it the physical therapy? Was it my changed diet recommended for MS? Was it my following **A Course in Miracles?** Was it psychotherapy? Was it yoga? Was it acupuncture? Was it taking any supplement that I thought had even a small chance of helping? Was it my loving and supportive wife? Was it my dedication to being a psychotherapist, which I love? Was it following the **personal power recommendations the archetypal images made in my dreams?** The answer was obvious.

Yes.

CHAPTER 1:
BEGINNING KEYS

Key 1: Dreams use the current day residue—events and materials from the dreamer's life. During the day there are innumerable events, objects, symbols, emotional events and personal stories from which the dreamer's subconscious can choose. The question before us is always, Why did the dreamer's subconscious focus on these particular items or events at this particular time? The dream almost always gives us far more than what we have been seeking. That is because dreams are a tremendous condensation that fits the maximum amount of meaning in a collage of often conflicting or strangely appearing symbols.

In dream interpretation, it is preferable for a client to report a recent long, detailed and complicated dream than to report the events of the last week. A long recent dream will report what has been going through the dreamer's mind. The dream will highlight the events, items, and relationships that are of immediate concern. It usually has to be decided whether the dream is simply giving a representation of what the current situation is or is giving a prediction of what is likely to happen. The subconscious is the latent eighty percent of the mind that has the broadest view of all the factors impinging upon the total situation.

This is why people can have a feeling about what they should decide to do, but cannot clearly articulate the reasons that they feel that a certain course of action is the best route to take. The person may be aware subconsciously of all the factors or likely factors, but conscious insight has not yet been achieved, so the dreamer cannot articulate the reasons behind the decisions. Let us take a look at a dream to get a feel for how some of these principles come into play. As will be discussed later, for both males and females, dreams use men as code to represent an action part of a dreamer's psyche, while women usually represent an emotional portion of the dreamer's mind.

DREAM 1A: A REINTEGRATION ORGY

A 42-year-old woman dreamt that three macho abusive men were searching for her. A village captured the three men and tied them up. The dreamer asked each of the abusive men if they were sorry for how they hurt her. Each of them had no regrets. Then she was in a school building that was being remodeled into a church. All around the church were traditional dolls, each having a candle in front of them. It was like a death vigil ceremony. Then she dreamt that there was a massive orgy taking place.

DREAM 1A—INTERPRETATION

This woman was married and divorced three times. Each relationship was a disaster where she was emotionally and physically abused. The parts of her subconscious that dealt with these three relationships were on repeat. They had learned nothing. We know this because these parts of her subconscious remained unchanged and had no regrets in the dream.

A church and a school were prominent because the dream was calling for new spiritual learning. The traditional dolls represented her traditional ideas of what a woman should be like. They were unchanging mannequins, easily manipulated by others. Each carried a candle because fire almost always signals a change or transformation. Fire means change because it transforms matter into energy. A vigil or spiritual ritual recognized that the passage or change was taking place.

The orgy of sex at the end indicated integration. Many male (male characters usually represent actions) and female (female characters usually represent emotions) aspects of her psyche were integrating. Her actions and emotions were becoming more congruent and consistent, so that they worked better together. To the dreamer, that simply meant that her actions (the men in the orgy) were coordinating or integrating with her emotions (the women in the orgy). That it was an orgy served to emphasize the massive changes that were occurring within her.

The degree of the sex typically indicates the degree of integration between actions and emotions occurring within the dreamer. Kissing, making out, heavy petting and sexual intercourse are increasingly stronger symbols that integration is beginning (kissing) or that integration was attained (sexual intercourse). The subconscious views healthy and consensual sex between males and females in a spirit of love as promoting the integration of the individual on an intrapsychic level. On the interpersonal level, sex promotes the interrelatedness of the couple.

CHAPTER 2:
MALE AND FEMALE,
MOM AND DAD

Key 2A: Male characters are most often used by the dream to indicate actions. Female characters most often are used by the dreamer's unconscious to represent emotions. This is not absolutely so, but it is usually the way things work out because of cultural trends over thousands of years.

Key 2B—Projection: A very important principle is that each character in the dream is a projection of a portion of the dreamer's subconscious. The character in the dream is first and foremost a part of the dreamer's unconscious. This first level of interpretation almost always has some validity. It is most tempting to interpret dream content as interpersonal interactions, but the interpreter cannot possibly know all the details needed to make accurate interpretations. The level of certainty rises from approximately fifty percent to as high as ninety percent when one considers each character or animal in the dream to be a symbolic part of the dreamer's subconscious, which fits into Carl Jung's panoramic view of dreams. This is a principle that the therapist must keep in mind consistently. Dreams are first and foremost intrapsychic conflicts, and are secondarily interpersonal conflicts. Dreams are frequently due to condensation of the maximum amount of meaning into the fewest possible symbols. Dream symbols are so packed with meaning that it is usually relatively easy to discern one of the three or more meanings the symbol represents.

Both Key 2A and Key 2B are illustrated in dream 1A. Let's look at dreams that illustrate all of the beginning principles discussed thus far.

DREAM 2A: THE FATHER INTROJECT

A 28-year-old accountant dreamt that his father handed him a knife. The dreamer thought the knife was too dull so he was planning to sharpen the knife. His father then grabbed the knife, broke it into little pieces, and spread out the pieces of what was left of the knife in front of the dreamer.

DREAM 2A—INTERPRETATION

Theories of mental health assume that the child absorbs and introjects images of his father and mother into his subconscious. These become the father introject and the mother introject, which become default-like guides to behavior when the person runs into a situation that they have not encountered before. The mental system goes on default and the person reviews their mother and father introjects to see if there is something of value there that they saw in the past that just might work in the new situation they encountered. Sometimes after reviewing introjects, the person then makes a statement in the present situation and then realizes "that sounds just like what my mother (or father) would have said."

The person's subconscious went on default, the unconscious introjects were reviewed, and a solution was proffered to the conscious, which the person accepted because some response is usually viewed as preferable to no response.

The father and mother introjects are usually constructed from biological mother and father introjects, but not necessarily so. The introject may be constructed from a kindly relative. The introject may also consist of an amalgamation of various people, such as an older good friend, an uncle, an aunt, a grandfather or grandmother, mentors or stepparents.

The father introject usually goes with the dreamer's actions. The mother introject usually goes with the dreamer's emotions. This is not absolutely so, but that is usually the way things go in dreams because the archetypes or patterns of thought handed down through the generations are based on hundreds, if not thousands, of years of culture.

In this dream, the father introject was telling the dreamer that he was working with a dull tool. The dreamer felt that his job as an accountant was very boring and dull. The dreamer thought he could make the job better by being the "sharpest knife in the drawer." The father introject destroyed the knife, which told the dreamer that there was no way for him to satisfactorily transform his job. On the basis of this dream, this young and talented man successfully pursued opening his own business.

DREAM 2B: THE MOTHER INTROJECT

The same 28-year-old accountant dreamt that his mother demanded that he take her to dinner. He ran to get the car. His mother sardonically laughed at him because he did not know where to take her.

DREAM 2B—INTERPRETATION

The dreamer tried to nurture himself and made his best efforts. In spite of this, he tended to emotionally belittle his efforts. He reported that his best efforts to achieve were almost never even acknowledged by his mother, which determined the formation of his mother introject. The dream was saying that he needed to reward himself emotionally. He should reward himself when he makes his best effort, even if it does not turn out. He would increase his chances of success if he was able to modify his mother introject so that he was not emotionally afraid to take risks because he feared punishment from his subconscious mother introject.

DREAM 2C: GETTING RID OF HANG-UPS

A 29-year-old woman dreamt that she and her mother were in an office apartment above a house. She could see the steps leading down to the house. She went to the basement of the house and was able to see into a closet that was very high in that its ceiling extended upward fifty feet. At the top, her mother was committing suicide by hanging herself with a rope. The dreamer tried to get a ladder to rescue her mother, but it was too late.

DREAM 2C—INTERPRETATION

This dream featured her mother introject. Movement down steps in a dream usually signifies movement into the unconscious, especially if it proceeds down to a basement. The dream was recommending that she give up following her mother introject. Although she made efforts to save emotions in her mother introject, her subconscious clearly wanted her to reject her mother's lethal emotions, which were instilled in the dreamer's mother introject. Her mother consistently ignored her and gave her bad and even poisonous advice as she was growing up.

DREAM 2D: KILLING MY EMOTIONS SO MUCH I CAN HARDLY MOVE

A 22-year-old man dreamt that he and a group of lawbreakers of which he was a member killed a beautiful blonde woman and decapitated her. He next saw himself with his father, trying to make their way through a crowd of potentially violent men. He was very afraid because the crowd was so dense that they made almost no progress.

DREAM 2D INTERPRETATION—A BIG DREAM INTERPRETATION

The dreamer had this dream many times before in his life. Dr. Carl Jung noted that some dreams were big dreams. Big dreams mean more than other dreams because they usually represent subconscious repeated attempts to either solve or warn about recurrent conflicts. A recurrent dream is virtually always a big dream. The subconscious is throwing out a warning that a major psychological conflict that occurred in the past is once again recurring in the dreamer's present life.

The dreamer was adrift since high school and could not find his way toward completing a college degree, getting a job, or being in a serious relationship. He was agoraphobic and left home with extreme difficulty. In the dream, the dream starts out, as dreams often do, by stating what is causing the habitual problem. The problem is that his **Shadow** (the crowd of lawbreakers) killed his emotions (the beautiful **Anima** woman). The father introject, which is a part of him, was unable to take effective action because of his multiple fears. Specifically, he emotionally lost his head so that he was unable to take effective action to make progress around his many fears (the crowd of violent men).

DREAM 2E: FACING MY FEARS, OR THANKS DAD

The same 22-year-old man (dream 2D) some weeks later dreamt that he and his father were in their backyard. The neighbors next door were having a large, raucous party in their backyard. The party was starting to spill over into the dreamer's backyard. The dreamer hesitated to say anything out of fear of reprisal. With his father's support, the dreamer finally decided to talk to the group of Mexicans spilling over into his backyard. The party people retreated to their own property. His father was proud of him.

DREAM 2E—INTERPRETATION

This dreamer was in therapy because he was agoraphobic and literally did not leave his parents' house. In therapy, the focus was on him taking risks and going out to begin his adult life. He now was working out, applying for jobs, and had started going to college. The Mexicans in the dream were calling for a more soulful response from him (the darker the skin, the more soul is being summoned). His father introject was the main action part of himself, which supported his taking action. The dream described his taking the necessary actions to set boundaries between himself and others. Knowing that he could do this reduced his fears dramatically. It set the basis for his taking action in his own life.

CHAPTER 3:
WATER IS SUBCONSCIOUS EMOTION

Key 3: Water is virtually always emotions and the subconscious. The ocean is the huge symbol of the primordial unconscious. Raging water, typhoons, and stormy seas represent turbulent emotions. Rain is typically depression, but it can be regenerative, as rain causes growth. Snow and ice are cold emotions. The ocean typically is the unconscious, land is conscious events, and the beach is the semiconscious or where the unconscious meets consciousness. A person strolling along an ocean beach in a dream is typically trying to sort out his or her conscious and unconscious issues.

DREAM 3A: SORTING OUT RELATIONSHIPS

A male college sophomore dreamt that he was resting on a beach with his girlfriend. They were looking at a beautiful seashell. Suddenly, they were transported to his bedroom. His girlfriend remained calm while he saw, on the distant wall in front of the bed, a witch-like image of his previous girlfriend. His previous girlfriend was subject to quite delusional bouts of bizarre behavior. He saw the girlfriend change into an alien and walk past him while his current girlfriend persevered in bed with him. She urged him to ignore the alien girlfriend and look at the seashell instead.

DREAM 3A—INTERPRETATION

The man lying on a beach implied that he was trying to consciously work on subconscious issues. The current girlfriend in the dream was the emotional part of himself that related to that girlfriend. The seashell is a treasure of the ocean, which indicated that he had treasure in his subconscious.

The emotional part of himself that related to his current girlfriend was calming him. He was being urged to ignore past distracting emotions while focusing on the treasures that were within his subconscious.

DREAM 3B: WHERE THE BUFFALO ROAM

A 38-year-old woman dreamt that she was swimming in the ocean with sharks on each side of her. The waves were high and tumultuous. She became increasingly alarmed and decided to swim as quickly as she could to a nearby island. When she made it to the island, she walked down the beach and found a dead buffalo that had washed ashore. She became at one with the spirit of the dead beast and she, as a spirit, went inland, feeling euphoric.

DREAM 3B—IN-TERPRETATION

She was severely physically and sexually abused as a child. She never realized how much the abuse affected her until she came to psychotherapy. She continued to put up with genuinely dangerous lovers and situations into adulthood, i.e., she literally learned to not notice the alarming danger of "swimming with the sharks." One also wants to remember that the sharks are a part of her. She had periods of anger that erupted unpredictably. As an abused child, her **Shadow** was stimulated far too often. The **Shadow's** anger was a protective response that tried to prevent any similar abuse from occurring in the future.

The ocean and its storms represented the abused emotions the dreamer was trying to navigate. She sought land, consciousness, which in this case was facilitated by her finally realizing that she needed to attend psychotherapy. She obtained a skilled therapist who helped her leave the past behind.

The dead buffalo represented the powerful instincts that were put in a situation where they never should have been. Buffalo are slow to react and frequently did not realize the danger they were in when they were being slaughtered on the plains. The days of her being the unwitting victim were over, but she took the spirit of strength from the powerful beast with her into a new day of consciousness.

DREAM 3C: A LITTLE SUPPORT CAN COST TOO MUCH

A 34-year-old woman dreamt she was outside walking past gigantic waterfalls with a huge dam nearby. The waterfalls and the dam were to the left of her. She came to stairs that went downward. She followed these downward steps until she came to a landing at the bottom. To her right were two staircases, each of which went upward. She inexplicably took the staircase that was narrower and more difficult to climb. She ended up at the Southern plantation-like home where she grew up. Everyone was old and stuffy and dressed aristocratically. She felt uncomfortable. She asked an educated younger, spiritual lady to please get her a drink of water. The lady got it for her, but informed her later that

the glass of water cost five hundred dollars that the dreamer had to pay now. The dreamer felt confused and somewhat betrayed.

DREAM 3C—INTERPRETATION

The gigantic waterfalls and nearby dam were reassuring her that she had a huge amount of emotional resources and unconscious or subconscious energy. The water being to the left indicated that the unconscious was involved. The dreamer was overweight and took the most difficult staircase to the right of her. The right is associated with conscious decisions and actions.

She recently decided not to go home to South Carolina, which was a hard decision for her. The dream was reaffirming her decision by indicating that going there would be difficult and stuffy. She asked for a drink of water at her home. She was asking for a small amount of emotional support from her home and family. The dream indicated that the support would be small and would cost her too much. The dreamer had a habit of paying dearly emotionally for small requests. Her boyfriend recently left her because he felt servile in the relationship. Believe it or not, she frequently asked him to get her a glass of water.

DREAM 3D: BREAKING THROUGH THE INTROJECTS

A 63-year-old woman dreamt that she was waving a saw in the air while her parents were in the distance watching her. She then saw herself breaking up ice by stomping on it on a lake. She was worried that she might break through the ice because she did not know if the ice was too thin.

DREAM 3D—INTERPRETATION

She was thinking of cutting off communication with her parents (thus the waving of the saw). Within her psyche, she felt the need to break away from the influence of her parental introjects, as her behavior was determined too much by past parental values. Ice is frozen water and therefore represents cold emotions. She felt this was risky because she risked being on "thin ice" (cold emotions) with her parents and internalized introjects if she exposed or broke through by using too aggressive actions (i.e., too much stomping).

CHAPTER 4:
EMOTIONS ARE THE
TIGER IN YOUR TANK

Key 4: Animals are unconscious or subconscious energy within the dreamer. Animals represent instinctive energy. They virtually always make a statement about how much energy is present and the quality of the energy, i.e., is it calm and soothing or frenetic and confusing?

DREAM 4A: THE TIGER TREADS WATER CALMLY

A 28-year-old woman dreamt that she was at her employer's house. She was in the backyard and saw a beautiful white tiger swimming in the pool very calmly. She looked deeply into the serene tiger's soulful eyes. She was amazed that the tiger was swimming, that he was calm, and that he was not attacking her.

DREAM 4A—INTERPRETATION

The dream occurred at her employer's house because of the "homey" feeling she had around her employer. Water invariably represents emotions. In particular, a swimming pool represents "man-made" emotions, i.e., emotions in response to other people, usually around home. Animals represent instinctive unconscious energy and are barometers in forecasting what type and quantity of emotion is likely to appear. The tiger represented strength, its white color indicating spirituality. The tiger was comfortable in the water, i.e., the dreamer was comfortable with her emotions and her ability to "stay afloat" within her emotions. The tiger was not attacking her because the dreamer no longer had panic attacks. She was feeling more spiritual and calmer with her perceptive sensitivity.

Dream 4B: Taking the Venom Out of Emotion

A 46-year-old man dreamt he was in his backyard. He netted a fish-like poisonous creature from the swimming pool. The creature was half fish and half snake. He eventually herded the creature out of his backyard and into an alley.

Dream 4B—Interpretation

Water is almost always emotion, with a swimming pool indicating that the emotion is in response to other people, that it is man-made, and that it is close to home. Aquatic creatures, such as fish, represent subconscious energy and resources. The snake in this dream was poisonous. Snakes often represent change and transformation because snakes are one of the few animals

that completely shed their skin. The dream indicated that he was using his emotional energy to change by directing his venom, his poisonous emotions and anger, away from home, where it could not hurt anyone.

DREAM 4C: JOINING THE RIVER OF LIFE

A 28-year-old woman dreamt that she had a long shag carpet in which fish were somehow living. She realized that the situation was not good for the fish and that they needed to go outside to larger waters. The dreamer then saw a river near her home and thought to herself that she should put the fish in the river, where they could live and love freely.

DREAM 4C—INTERPRETATION

This woman had agoraphobia and could not get herself to leave home because she was afraid she would be hurt. The dream was telling her directly that she had unconscious resources and energy that were squandered in the house in a situation that was not letting her live her life. The dream indicated that she needed to get outside the home and join the flow of emotions comprising the river of life. As Hermann Hesse noted in his outstanding Buddha book, Siddhartha, "life is indeed a river."

CHAPTER 5:
THOSE FURRY LOVING PETS

Key 5: Pets, such as cats and dogs, usually represent affectionate feelings. It is not great love; rather, it is how you feel toward a family cat or dog. They are held in high esteem because they listen well, they do not talk back, and they are furry. What more could a person want! Their unconditional positive regard is well earned. Cats tend to be positive female affectionate feelings because of their sensuous, intelligent and independent feline nature. The affectionate female feels free to express her positive emotions. Dogs tend to represent male affectionate feelings, as dogs are famous for being protective and even heroic in defense of their owners. Affectionate feelings propel men toward using the Heroic Masculine, which is the positive part of masculinity that would literally die for his loved ones or his country.

DREAM 5A: STOP PULLING THE CAT'S TAIL

A 58-year-old man dreamt that he took his pet cat to a veterinarian because there was something wrong with the cat's tail. Then an overriding voice commanded him to "Go See a Doctor."

DREAM 5A—INTERPRETATION

Cats are family pets that represent female affectionate feelings. The dreamer going to a veterinarian signified that he needed a doctor who understood how to work with basic instincts or basic energy. The idea that there was something wrong with the cat's tail implied that he might be mishandling family females. The tail is located near the first chakra which, according to philosophy from

India, is related to family or tribal loyalty. You are sitting on your first chakra which is the most basic and instinctive energy. A cat's tail can be injured and the cat can be annoyed by someone pulling its tail, i.e., the dream was dramatizing his concern over how he might be mistreating his wife and adult daughter. The admonition to "Go See a Doctor" clearly referred to seeing a doctor (in this case a therapist with a doctorate) for treatment of his emotional handling of his family. He was a good father and family man whose subconscious concern for his family led him to therapy.

DREAM 5B: HURT FEELINGS

A 22-year-old man dreamt that his favorite pet cat was stuck in a small culvert in the ground and was in danger of being flooded. He could see only the cat's face and had to struggle to free it from the torrential water. He noticed that the cat was seriously hurt. When he took the cat home, he told his mother that he was going to take the cat to the veterinarian. His mother did not want him to take the cat to the doctor.

DREAM 5B—INTERPRETATION

Cats in this case represented his affections for women. Water is emotion and the action taking place near a culvert that was underground indicated that subconscious emotion was involved. He had recently had a string of relationships, each of which lasted only about three or four months. The wounded cat represented the degree to which his affection for women was hurt. He thought he should go to therapy to resolve his reluctance to try again, but the mother introject part of his emotions was skeptical. This client did decide to continue therapy after this dream helped to explicate the main source of his current emotional pain.

DREAM 5C: PROTECT YOURSELF FIRST

A 39-year-old man dreamt he was a member of a hunting party, each of whom had a shotgun. First, they shot a squirrel. Next they shot a skunk. They then tried to shoot a Dalmatian dog, but only wounded it. He covered the dog and protected it.

DREAM 5C—INTERPRETATION

He was trying to sort himself out in therapy. In the dream, he first rid himself of some of the "squirrel" part that got him into trouble with other people. He then got rid of the sarcastic part of himself (the skunk) intent on making other people stink.

Dalmatians are famous for being dogs that ran with fire engines in times past. Fire is transforming, since it changes matter into energy. It is a luminous (giving off light) indicator of change. Dogs are frequently seen as protective and firemen are the living essence of the **Heroic Masculine**, as they put their lives on the line for others. The dream ended by pointing out that his **Heroic Masculine** was wounded by his past actions of thinking that he was saving certain women. The dream pointed out that part of his psyche was wounded, but not killed, and it was now time for him to protect that well-meaning part of himself.

DREAM 5D: PROTECT YOUR INNER PET

A 28-year-old man dreamt that he was roaming the streets at night because it was his job to shoot stray dogs. At one point he came across three puppies in an alley in a small kennel. He stomped the dogs to death with his boots. He felt sick and disgusted with himself.

DREAM 5D—INTERPRETATION

The dream was strongly saying that he had to get rid of subconscious and wild impulses. The dogs represented instinct or the id, which was literally saying that he had to control himself, that it was his job to get rid of impulses that should not have a home within him. Family pets usually represent our affectionate feelings. Pets listen well, do not talk back, and are sensuous. These qualities deserved more admiration! His behavior was literally destroying his affectionate feelings. It was often his experience that women were attracted to him because he liked new, exciting activities and people, but he never settled down and committed himself to anyone. Thus, he was never experiencing a relationship with commitment, which made him feel sad and alienated from his feelings.

ADDENDUM TO PETS KEY 5:
PETS CAN BE MORE
THAN AFFECTION

Pet dogs and cats can represent our affections, but one wants to remember that they are complex animals that represent certain instincts. An example would be a fairy tale by Hans Christian Anderson. Fairy tales and legends are considered to be primary expressions of the collective unconscious. Fairy tales are reservoirs of a culture's basic subconscious or unconscious beliefs. They are exemplars of a culture's messages to the individual's subconscious and constantly influence individual dreams. This Hans Christian Anderson fairy tale was considered as a dream in an extended and interesting interview of Jungian analyst Tom Elsner by David Van Nuys, Ph.D. in podcast interview #293 for www.ShrinkRapRadio. com. It is presented below as a dream, with my interpretation largely corresponding with Tom Elsner's interpretation.

DREAM 5E: THE HEROIC MASCULINE MANAGES EMOTIONS TO COLLECT HIS TREASURE

The dream started out with a soldier who was released from service and traveling down a road. He met a witch or hag who asked him to do a task for her. She indicated to the soldier that she wanted him to retrieve buried treasure. Part of the treasure was a "tinder box." A tinder box consisted of a flint or rock in a steel box along with easily flammable dried particles of wood, which were used to start fires prior to the invention of matches. She emphasized that she especially and specifically wanted the tinder box above all else.

The treasure was guarded by a series of increasingly larger and more ferocious dogs. The first dog guarded a store of copper, the second dog guarded a store of silver, and the third and largest ferocious dog guarded a store of gold. As the value of the treasure increased, the size of the dogs' eyes increased from the size of teacups to the size of a wagon wheel. She noted that the only way to get past the dogs was to use a magical apron that she gave to him to sedate the dogs while he stole their treasure. She guided him to the underworld by lowering him through a hollow tree.

The magical apron worked as the witch described and sedated the fearsome dogs. The soldier gained the copper, which he subsequently left behind to carry all the silver he could, which was eventually left behind so he could carry the most valuable gold home. While retrieving the gold, he also found the coveted tinder box. When he returned to the hollow tree, the witch looked down at him and wanted him to give her the tinder box. The soldier cleverly told her that he would give her the tinder box after she pulled him to the surface. When emerging from the tree, the soldier drew his sword and cut off the head of the evil witch.

The soldier eventually used his renewed powers to free a beautiful princess imprisoned in a castle. And he found out why the evil witch wanted the tinder box so much. Whenever he was in trouble, he could conquer his adversaries by striking a flame with the tinder box. When he did so, the fearsome dogs appeared to save the day. Needless to say, the soldier and the beautiful princess lived happily ever after.

DREAM 5E—INTERPRETATION

The soldier represented the **Heroic Masculine** since a soldier serves and protects and is willing to die for a greater purpose. The witch was representative of the negative mother complex, which wants to use the **Heroic Masculine** for its own purpose. The underworld or underground that the soldier was lowered to represented the subconscious, which underlies conscious reality. The dogs represented his protective animal instinct, which is especially powerful in the **Heroic Masculine**.

As a dream, the dreamer was being reassured that there was treasure in his or her subconscious. The problem was that the dreamer was being too protective or defensive, to the point that the inner treasures could not be used. The solution was the apron, which is pragmatic emotionality with a focus on getting things done without getting dirty (this positive common-sense emotionality is protective of the dreamer).

The tinder box starts fire. Fire is a symbol of change or transformation, as it converts matter into energy. The tinder box eventually represented controlled emotionality in service to the ego, which he summoned at will, as he was then able to properly use his inner animal instincts to accomplish positive goals. The eyes of the dogs became larger with each succeeding treasure, which indicates growing awareness. The eyes are indeed the windows to the soul. Such retention of control destroyed the negative mother complex, which is why the witch was killed. Instead of serving evil and manipulative purposes, the soldier is transformed into freeing positive feminine emotionality, the captive princess.

The dream started with a symbol of integration, a tree. The dream indicated that to integrate, he had to work on his subconscious to recover inner resources, which he guarded too closely. Remember that all persons or animals in a dream are part of the dreamer's psyche. The fairy tale dream ended with his living happily ever after because his **Heroic Masculine** was now serving positive emotionality as he integrated with the positive feminine energy of the princess.

CHAPTER 6:
FLY HIGH, SKY PILOT

Key 6: Flying is a big deal. Flying is virtually always significant in a dream. It generally signifies a time where the dreamer is feeling extremely and personally powerful. How the dreamer is flying in the dream is important. The more active the form of flight, the more significant the dream is in portending changes in the dreamer's life. The following list ranks the forms of flight in terms of the strength of the symbol, with the symbols becoming stronger and more significant as one goes down the list:

- Jumping high like your shoes are made of Silly Putty
- Floating in a balloon
- Floating in the air alone like a balloon
- Hang gliding
- Flying a biplane
- Flying a propeller aircraft
- Flying a jet
- Flying like Superman

It has been my experience as a therapist that someone who saw him or herself flying through the air like Superman, with no visible means of support, was likely to experience major life changes within the next eighteen months. This agrees with at least some out- of-body travelers who regard flying in a dream as being close to having an out-of-body experience. I have never had an out-of-body experience. I am most focused on having in-body experiences. Dreams can be used to escape reality, but they are better used to explicate reality. It seems that flying in a symbolic dream is more likely to be beneficial in providing needed information to the dreamer.

DREAM 6A: A RECURRENT FLYING DREAM

A 23-year-old woman had a recurring dream that she first dreamt when she was eight years old. She was riding a flying unicorn over Niagara Falls and she flew down near the bottom of the falls. The water was full of orca whales. She leveled out safely and flew on with exhilaration.

DREAM 6A—INTERPRETATION

Not all dreams are created equal. Dr. Carl Jung, the master of dream interpretation, noted that some dreams are "big" because they have special (or luminous in his terminology) meaning for the dreamer that is likely to be especially important for the dreamer's life. Recurrent dreams are fraught with meaning and are considered "big" because the dreamer faces a repetitive conflict throughout life, which the unconscious is trying to help the dreamer resolve. Flying dreams imply that things are going to rapidly change, that things will start flying, in the near future. Her parents divorced when she was eight years old. Water invariably represents the unconscious or emotion. There was much turbulence that ended in a waterfall, which represented the confusion she felt as a child during the divorce of her parents. The situation was a "downer," which was the reason for the waterfall.

She had massive animals that were flying or were in the water (her unconscious). The dream was reassuring her that she had massive emotional resources that she could draw upon to deal with massive, turbulent, depressing personal situations. Animals in dreams represent instinctive energy. She had a magical imagination powered by a flying horse or unicorn, as well as the huge and multiple whale energy in her subconscious. This dream recurs when she needs to be reassured that she can weather confusing and stressful emotional situations.

DREAM 6B: LANDING OR GROUNDING A RELATIONSHIP

A 24-year-old girl dreamt that she was on an airplane with her boyfriend. She was dressed as a spy wearing a trench coat. Her boyfriend was dressed similarly. Three women on the plane were also dressed as spies. The plane was on fire. She looked out the window and saw a sandbar in the ocean. On the sandbar were dozens of previously crashed airplanes. She next saw herself and her boyfriend on the sandbar. They were safely on the sandbar and the airplane was parked on the sandbar, undamaged. They were having fun in the water near the beach. There were dolphins swimming and playing near the sandbar.

DREAM 6B—INTERPRETATION

She and her boyfriend were shadowy figures, which indicated that their **Shadows,** the part of the subconscious that looks out for and defends self-interests, was involved in changing their lives. Three is an unstable number in relationships and indicates that things will change. The three women indicated that her emotions were especially involved in the change that was occurring. Flight is often spiritually significant in dreams. The fire signified that major spiritual change was occurring, as fire transforms matter into energy. They were being forced to land in a situation about which they were very wary.

The woman had fears that the relationship would not work, which is signified by the pile of previously crashed planes, which represented previous breakups. Those relationships ended when the people decided to live together. This couple not only survived the landing with the airplane intact, but were having fun, which is emphasized by the positive and playful dolphin energy. Fish are unconscious or subconscious resources or energy that can be used by the dreamer. This dream was reassurance that they could land with their relationship intact.

DREAM 6C: SHOCK THE MONKEY

A 43-year-old man dreamt that he was trying to soar with a hang glider that allowed him to literally take flight by hanging on to a steel bar while the kite-like apparatus propelled him through the air. He dreamt that there were numerous monkeys having sex all around him, interfering with the flight. A huge sexual orgy of monkeys surrounded his attempt to fly.

DREAM 6C—INTERPRETATION

Animals in dreams most often represent basic instincts. Monkeys are the animal most closely resembling human beings. The dream was saying, in very graphic terms, that his sexual impulses were interfering with his making progress and "soaring" in life. The man was promiscuous without involving his emotions, which was harmful to relationships and to his psyche. In no uncertain terms, the dream was telling him to quit monkeying around.

DREAM 6D: AWAKEN THE SLEEPING GIANT

A 37-year-old man dreamt that he was running to catch a plane. There were two seaplanes parked near the water. He bypassed the first plane, which was a modern jet made for executives. He saw the pilot was in the plane, but could not make out his features. The second plane was weighed down by an incredible pile of baggage being loaded onto it. The flight attendants paid no attention to him, even though he could not find a seat for himself on the plane.

The dream then shifted to the house where he grew up. To one side was an outside stairway that went down to the basement. His brother went down into the basement and came back screaming in fright because of what he saw there. The dreamer went down into the basement and saw a beautiful, restful basement with the furniture appearing abnormally large. His father was sleeping in the recliner chair.

Dream 6D—Interpretation

Flying is among the several things that indicate a spiritual journey with major implications for the dreamer's life is taking place. Water represents emotion. The dreamer saw the possibilities of two emotional flights for his life. The first involved the modern notion of climbing up the ladder of success. He did not see the pilot because that part of his psyche was not fully developed. The second plane was overloaded with baggage, which represented his "baggage" from the past. He felt unrecognized and ignored by people who should have been helping him.

The second part of the dream gave clues to the structure of his unconscious and also offered a solution. He had an older brother, whom his emotionally abusive father criticized relentlessly. This brother became a dependent alcoholic. The dream gave an indication that his brother had horrors instilled in his subconscious by his father. The furniture was abnormally big, as it would appear to a child, which assures us that the dream was talking about deep subconscious processes. His father actually treated the dreamer himself relatively well.

The father in the dream represented the action part of his psyche, which is too subconscious (the father is sleeping) to be effective. The dream was pointing to the huge unused reservoir of action energy in his father introject that was going untapped. He was reluctant to use his assertive father introject because of the harm he saw his father inflict emotionally upon his brother. In his life, he found that when he used his assertiveness, it helped him in both his marriage and at work. He was subconsciously worried about becoming aggressive like his father, which is why he preferred, to his detriment, to let the giant sleep.

Dream 6E: Let the Inner Boy Fly

A 28-year-old male graduate student dreamt that he was surrounded on the university campus by hundreds of nearly lifeless automaton students. They were crowding him, and he was having extreme difficulty getting to where he wanted to go. Suddenly he saw a male student who resembled himself floating in the air about three stories above the dreamer. The floating student appeared to be lying with his back to the dreamer as he floated in midair.

The dreamer did everything he could to awaken the student who seemed to be slumbering while he casually and gently floated in the air. He finally yelled, "Wake up!" The sleeper immediately came to life and started flying around the campus. The flying student had no obstacles and appeared to be having the time of his life. Later, the police questioned the flying student in his dorm room, but did not arrest him because he had really done nothing wrong.

DREAM 6E—INTERPRETATION

This graduate student studied obsessively and excessively. He made no room in his life for social or leisure activities. His lifeless, obsessive approach to life was interfering with his completing projects, as he was acquiring "analysis paralysis." He obsessively and compulsively recopied his work, which caused his academic progress on his dissertation to be extremely slow. Each character in the dream represented a part of the dreamer's psyche. The "hundreds of students" indicated too much of his psyche was devoted to robotic behavior that was interfering with his academic progress (as he metaphorically could not get anywhere on campus).

The dream recommended that he wake up and go above and beyond his compulsive tendencies. There were serious consequences to his flying. His conscience or superego, represented by the police, indicated mainly that there was nothing wrong with his flying (he was not arrested by the police). On the basis of this dream, the dreamer decided to loosen up somewhat, have fun in his studies to some degree, and to develop more of a social life. His grades subsequently improved as he stopped wasting time in the fruitless practice of recopying his academic work.

CHAPTER 7:
THE VOICE OF
THE UNCONSCIOUS

Key 7: An overriding and often commanding voice in a dream that is short and to the point is the unconscious talking directly to the dreamer.

The unconscious or subconscious sometimes simply sees the situation so clearly, and the dreamer is so unaware of the repetitive mistakes that are being made, that the unconscious gives up all pretense and gives the advice or remedy directly to the dreamer because the dreamer had not listened previously. It is the subconscious dramatically and directly commanding the dreamer's attention with a voice that says, "Listen to me."

DREAM 7A: NO MORE MERCY KILLINGS

A 38-year-old executive dreamt that there were two squirrels on the side of a highway. One of the squirrels was hit by a car and died. The other squirrel carried the dead squirrel to an altar, where his spiritual and religious aunt offered prayers to God for the squirrel.

The scene shifted to the dreamer being a commander in the army. Word came down from high command, stated in a deep, overriding voice, that there were to be "NO MORE MERCY KILLINGS."

The dream shifted again to him piloting a car that was going too fast and careened over the median dividing the four lane highway.

Dream 7A—Interpretation

The executive was a kind, spiritual, humorous and moral man. He also had an exceedingly funny and "squirrelly" side. The two squirrels represented the two sides of his nature. The dream indicated that part of his squirrelly nature had been killed even though he was trying to follow the "high way," the moral and spiritual way of living (which is why the spiritual aunt, prayers and an altar were involved).

He recently was almost forced, because employees took it somewhat better from him, to lay off about twenty percent of his company's employees. The people were low producers who eventually were going to lose their jobs, anyway. Because of this, he rationalized that his firings were actually "mercy killings" to shorten the pain of prolonged negative evaluation and periods of decreasing performance. He no longer wanted to be the person to deliver the news that they were fired, even though he was being paid an enormous bonus for doing the firings. Under the circumstances, he felt guilty that he was making "a killing."

He wanted to change his career. In the dream his spiritual and moral emotional side (his favorite aunt) was praying to God to save his fun and squirrelly nature. His conscience was framed by the soul order from "high command" in the form of the unconscious hyper- powered voice that he was not to participate in the distasteful "mercy killings."

The dream gave a final warning that he might be careening toward disaster, that he was crossing the line (the highway median) to propel his career forward.

Dream 7B: Advice from the Soul

A 28-year-old man employed as a social worker dreamt of a Holy Roller preacher with a swollen face and a bleeding head wound delivering a sermon about how the dreamer should expect more from other people. The preacher emphasized that other people should obey the commandments and not just respond to your efforts to help them. The dreamer liked the preacher in some way because he was committed to the truth, even if he was rigid and staunch in his beliefs. The dreamer was told that the women seated next to him were questionable, but he nevertheless felt there was a ninety percent chance that they were all right. The preacher rebuked him with a commanding and overriding voice, which impressed upon the dreamer that he was to have "no contact" with women who act questionably. It reminded him of the recent no contact order dictated to him by a judge. He was getting divorced from a woman after only ten months because she was a Russian who married him so that she would not be deported.

Dream 7B—Interpretation

Each character in the dream represented a part of the dreamer's subconscious. The dreamer was a spiritual man whose father died when he was eight years old. From that point on, "God the Father" became his psychological father. He added God the Father to his father introject, which he relied upon for masculine guidance. The dreamer was naive regarding women, to the point that he was often taken advantage of in relationships. He was warned that he must expect more from other people, especially women who may have malevolent intentions, even if they showed up in church. The dreamer nevertheless persisted in his over-optimism that ninety percent of questionable women were fine.

The spiritual side of himself had been mistreated and wounded in the past by sociopathic or mentally ill women. In the dream his subconscious wanted him to commit himself to the unequivocal command that he have no contact with the type of women who harmed him in the past. Dreamers must pay particular attention to overriding voices in dreams because these most frequently represent serious and direct warnings from the dreamer's unconscious or soul. The dreamer ignores such warnings at his or her own peril.

DREAM 7C: DAD TRIES TO HELP

A 52-year-old woman dreamt she was being asked by her father to give him three minutes to let him tell her something. He then told her that her favorite aunt had a blood test that indicated that she had cancer. An overriding encompassing voice proclaimed, "She did too much for others and not enough for herself." The aunt was a lively and vivacious person who consistently put her needs last to please others.

DREAM 7C—INTERPRETATION

Three people in a relationship is an unstable dynamic where almost always one of the three feels like an outsider. Things are going to change. The dream announced, as dreams will do, that this dream was going to be about changing her actions because the message was delivered by her father introject, which typically represents the action part of a person (not necessarily so, but that is usually the way it falls out after thousands of years of culture). Red and blood are associated with the first chakra in the East, which is the seat of family or tribal allegiance (you are sitting on your first chakra). Her father introject was telling her, with a dramatic overriding voice, that one should not neglect personal needs too much for the sake of others. Cancer is often contracted by people who are too nice to the extent that their immune system does not recognize the parasitic invader. The immune system therefore does not dispose of the invader, which is catastrophic. The overriding voice indicated that it was a message straight from her unconscious, higher self or soul—whichever, as these terms are more or less referring to the same thing.

Chapter 8:
The Soul Has No
Beginning and No End

Key 8: Fully rounded and circular objects are symbols of the soul because they have no beginning and they have no end.

Dream 8A: Take Me Higher and Light My Fire

A 38-year-old woman dreamt that she was dancing on the edge of the circumference of a huge tambourine which was high in the air. The dreamer caught fire.

Dream 8A—Interpretation

This dream has many spiritual elements to it. Dancing, singing and flying are among the most spiritual events that can occur in a dream. This whole dream was a metaphor and warning to the dreamer. Circular objects are frequently associated with the soul, as they have no beginning and they have no end. The dream clearly warned the dreamer that dancing too close to the edge risked the dreamer getting burned out. Fire is a major symbol of transformation, as it changes matter into energy. Fire demands change and change now. The dreamer is too high in the air. She is too "airy" to have realistic contact with bodily feelings. On the basis of the above dream, she decided to decrease her work schedule.

Dream 8B: The Circle Must Be Modified, Dad

A 24-year-old man dreamt that men that he was close to in life were repeatedly forcing him to wear a wedding band that was gaudily and over-jeweled and a total horror to the eye. Over time he was given rings that each male donor had owned and worn. The last donor was his father who gave him his old ring. He always felt obligated to wear that ring, but was completely unhappy about it.

Dream 8B—Interpretation

A ring is a circle. Circles represent the soul because they have no beginning and no end. Rings in particular represent a soulful commitment, in this case to his fiancée. He was getting married to a beautiful and intelligent athletic woman who rocked his world. That rings are worn on the hand meant he was committing himself to working (physical work is accomplished largely with the hands) toward a soulful relationship. He did not want the totally traditional relationship, which he and his wife–to-be viewed as overdone and garish (like the overly ornate ring).

Each character in the dream represented another masculine part of himself that he wanted to honor and toward which he felt some residual loyalty. Nevertheless, he wanted to modify his symbol of commitment and not do things "the same old, overdone, standard way." He was respecting past parts of himself, but wanted to get beyond feeling obligated to do what others expected. He felt that what he was led to believe in the past needed to grow into a new kind of commitment.

DREAM 8C: HELP ME HELP YOU

A 46-year-old man dreamt that he and his girlfriend went to a hospital. They entered a hospital ward where the patient beds were all arranged in a circle with their feet facing the inside of the circle. He and his girlfriend were examining the bottoms of the patients' feet.

DREAM 8C—INTERPRETATION

The dream was telling him that, critical to the healing of their relationship and the healing of his soul, is that he be emotionally supportive (his girlfriend in the dream is an emotional part of himself). We know the dream is talking about healing because the dream used a hospital, which is a place of healing. The fact that the patient beds were arranged in a circle indicated that healing soul work was involved, as circles have no beginning and no end. The dream represented a super condensation because it addressed the issue both within his psyche and inter-personally or socially. That is, the dream indicated that he would benefit from being emotionally supportive and from receiving emotional support from his girlfriend. Additionally, they were examining the soles ("souls") of the patients' feet. Support was involved because feet are part of the apparatus that literally supports us and helps get us through life.

DREAM 8D: ROUND AND ROUND

A 66-year-old woman dreamt that she went to a grocery store with a tall, dark, handsome man who helped her find cans of food. She saw herself trying to open the can by going round and round the circle at the top of the can.

DREAM 8D—INTERPRETATION

A grocery store sells items that nurture you. A can contains preserved food from the past. Circles often indicate soul work because they have no beginning and no end. The handsome man was a positive action part of herself, the **Heroic Masculine**, was urging her to take care of herself. She was ruminating, going round and round, regarding which experiences from the past she should choose to preserve that would be nurturing to her. She was deciding which experiences from the past she wanted to open herself to because they nurtured her.

CHAPTER 9:
MAJOR SYMBOLS OF
TRANSFORMATION

Key 9: Fire and snakes are major symbols of transformation and change. Fire transforms matter into energy. Snakes are one of the few animals that completely shed their skin.

DREAM 9A: IT'S LONELY AT THE TOP

A 44-year-old woman dreamt that she was in a car in a parking lot near work. Her best friend was driving. Her best friend backed the car up, but came to an abrupt stop because the parking lot ended. They were in a parking lot of one hundred yards by one hundred yards that was in the sky and supported by a precipitous strand of earth. She next saw herself standing alone in the middle of the parking lot, crying over her situation. Her emotionally strong friend was now at the top of a stairway with the car. She thought to herself that the ride down would be rough, but that they would make it.

The dream then shifted to her being at work with a gigantic computer screen in front of her. A different and "nice" friend, who would do anything for anybody, was helping her find an account. The dreamer believed they would find the account. The dream then shifted to where the dreamer realized she now had to save her nice friend, who was refueling at a gas station and was unaware of a nearby growing, threatening volcano. She then saw herself and her mother totally surrounded by a metallic and silver garage attached to the house where she grew up. She felt fortunate that the garage door was able to open to let them out.

DREAM 9A—INTERPRETATION

She was a career woman totally focused upon her career. After being abused physically by her father, and then later by an ex-husband, she was emotionally withdrawn from others. She focused all of her energy on her work. In the first part of the dream, she was literally stranded in her job at the top of the world. The dream reassured her that she had a strong part of her psyche that would be able to become grounded. It promised that it would be a rough ride, but that she could make it.

In the second part of the dream, she was literally trying to account for losing the "nice" part of herself. She then realized that she needed to change, which was symbolized by the fire that goes with a volcano (fire transforms matter into energy). Volcanoes typically represent suppressed anger, which can erupt at any time. She wanted to refuel, to give energy to the nice part of herself, which was inhibited by her focus on corporate climbing.

The last part of the dream represented the part of her psyche, the mother introject, that was willing to do anything for others, to emotionally give undeserving others anything they wanted. She literally would give them what they wanted on a silver platter, much the way her mother kowtowed to her tyrannical father. The dream then reassured her that she could open the door to get away from the behavior she had learned from her mother.

DREAM 9B: HUNGRY FOR CHANGE

The night before attending his first session of therapy, a 23-year-old man dreamt that he ran up a hill to feed three large, famished snakes.

DREAM 9B—INTERPRETATION

After hearing this dream during his first session of therapy, I told him that he really wanted to change. His reaction was intense and immediate. He burst into tears. This dream was a condensation of several factors. The number three signifies change. Snakes frequently represent change because of their regular transformations of completely shedding their skin. The fact that the snakes were exceedingly hungry and his willingness to run up a hill indicated the intensity of his desire.

DREAM 9C: INCORPORATING CHANGE INTO HIS LIFE

A 46-year-old man dreamt that he saw two snakes facing each other. One was a rattlesnake and the other was a cobra. He thought the cobra was the stronger of the two snakes. They were getting ready to lunge at one another. When they did lunge, the cobra completely swallowed the rattlesnake.

DREAM 9C—INTERPRETATION

He had a brief marriage when he was eighteen. He currently was having marital difficulties. His wife wanted him to exhibit sustained change of character.

He recently did something he had never done before. He had never forgiven his first wife for cheating on him, which led to the divorce. He had recently seen her on the Internet. He meditated on his feelings, and much to his surprise, he forgave her in his heart. He and his first wife had a brief and positive exchange of emails, which ended with the sentiment that the past was over. They wished each other well and said goodbye. He felt a major emotional breakthrough.

Snakes are a primal symbol of change and transformation because they are one of the few animals to completely shed their skin. The rattlesnake represented the change in his instinctive feelings toward his first wife. This forgiveness of his first wife was a major change that led to an improved relationship with his second wife.

The cobra represented his current, stronger instinctive feelings toward his present wife. The change of feeling toward his first wife was completely incorporated into his feelings toward his present wife, thus improving them as well. That is why the cobra swallows the rattlesnake. His improvement of relationship feelings was being fully incorporated (swallowed whole) to improve his current marriage.

CHAPTER 10:
THE SHADOW – THE SOURCE
OF CHANGE

Key 10: The Shadow is the main source of change.

I had a psychoanalytic professor in graduate school who did hypnotherapy with multiple personalities (Watkins, 1982). His theory was that we are all like multiple personalities in a sense. We are one way at work, another way at church, and are very different with our parents and with our lovers, for example. All the different parts of the psyche are in communication with one another, so that there is one overall executive personality that decides which portion of the psyche to use in a given situation. People become multiple personalities when they build hard, rigid and inflexible walls between the different parts of the psyche, so that it feels like different personalities.

Under hypnosis, the good professor would elicit and separate the various personalities. He literally talked to the different personalities and saw himself as doing family therapy within one person. The goal was to negotiate with the different parts of the psyche, so that they eventually accepted each another and the person would integrate and function as one personality.

During the course of this process, there would always be at least one surly and aggressive part that was focused upon self-survival. This part would be completely rejected by many parts of the psyche because of its disagreeable and selfish nature. Being brilliant, the good professor initially thought, early in his work, that it would be best to try to eliminate the **Shadow**. When this was attempted, the results were disastrous. Without the **Shadow**, what usually remained was a weak, namby-pamby, goody-two-shoes person, who could not get anything accomplished. He realized then that the **Shadow** does something very basic for the person. We think of it as containing aggressive impulses, but you also use the **Shadow** to get projects finished in your academic, business or personal life. One uses the **Shadow** in any sort of competition or desire to accomplish a goal. The **Shadow** is literally one's "get up and go."

My professor realized that one should not eliminate the **Shadow**. The **Shadow** needed to be integrated into the total personality. The **Shadow** was not dangerous as long as other parts of the psyche kept it from going too far.

We think of the **Shadow** as containing raw, aggressive instincts, but that is not all. The **Shadow** also contains parts of our psyche that we are not aware of or have put aside. If one decided not to become a priest, there is a priest in his or her **Shadow**.

Change most often comes about by accepting a part of ourselves that was previously rejected. This previously rejected part resides in the **Shadow**. We most often run away from the **Shadow** because it consists partially of frightening and/or previously rejected parts of ourselves. We have recurring dreams of being chased by our **Shadow** because it keeps trying to tell us that we could benefit from some subconscious resource located in the **Shadow**. We often need to turn around and face the pursuing **Shadow** to see what it is trying to offer. The **Shadow** is trying to get our attention because it wants to offer a part of itself that would be useful in one's current conflicts. It takes tremendous courage to face your **Shadow**, which explains why people have difficulty changing basic and underlying ways of functioning.

Change usually comes about because the person decided to put some portion of their psyche back in the **Shadow** or because the person decided to use a part of the **Shadow** because it is useful in a certain situation. Previously ignored parts of the psyche regain priority, while previously dominant parts of the psyche are diminished. We are not creating new parts that never existed or were not within the dreamer's potential. Virtually every part of our personality can be used for good in some situation in life. Having access to all parts of our personality promotes adaptability and versatility and improves personal functioning.

The **Shadow** is only dangerous when other structures are not available to positively direct its behavior. If one is not in contact at all with his or her **Shadow**, there is danger that it may become frustrated and take over the personality because the rest of the person is not considering the **Shadow's** input. The **Shadow** can be dangerous in this circumstance because reasonable limits are not being put upon it by other subconscious entities. When you've had it up to your ears in frustration, the **Shadow** will remove you from the situation by whatever means are available. This accounts for the situations where you did something in your own best interest in such a dramatic way that later you can hardly believe you did it. The **Shadow** is protective in focusing on self-survival and the person's own best self-interests.

DREAM 10A: TRUSTING THE SHADOW

A 38-year-old woman dreamt that she ran to a house. She was thinking of moving into the house, which was empty. The house had a large fortified steel gate in front. A shadowy dark figure sat on the front steps. She was wary of the figure. She was wondering if it was safe to open the gate.

DREAM 10A—INTERPRETATION

This was an early therapy dream. Early therapy dreams are much more likely to communicate the structure of the dreamer's subconscious to the therapist. A house can represent the dreamer to some extent because it is the structure out of which one lives. (The close association between houses and dreamers seems to be especially true for women, which is probably due to thousands of years of culture.) She was in therapy to figure out what to put in her life (her house.) That the house is empty signified that she was quite open and had a minimum of preconceived ideas. Her **Shadow** was sitting on the steps of the house. If a client changes, it is almost always due to his or her deciding to utilize some part of the **Shadow**. He can change by using a part of his **Shadow** he did not use before, or he can put a part of his personality back into the **Shadow**, or both. The therapist is not going to help the client develop a brand new part of himself; rather, the person prioritizes parts of himself and decides which parts of the psyche are going to be active. We do not create something entirely new in psychotherapy. We simply reshuffle the deck regarding which parts of the personality are going to be used according to the life situation. Parts of the personality may be used that were almost never used before, but the potential for that part always resided within the person.

We mostly do not trust the **Shadow** since we have rejected many parts of ourselves that reside there. We have difficulty believing that there is a part of our **Shadow**, either known or unknown, that may be useful in our lives.

So the dreamer was deciding whether it was safe to work with the **Shadow**. If it is going to be meaningful therapy, the **Shadow** will be involved in reshuffling the deck of the many parts of the client's personality.

DREAM 10B: LEAVE THE CHILD BE

A 32-year-old woman dreamt that she was a bartender in a twenty-story house. She was running through the house furiously, serving alcohol to the multitude of guests within the house. She was chased in the house by a dark shadowy force that eventually stole her four-year-old daughter. There was a crowd of elderly people who looked like her emotionally supportive grandparents shouting and protesting the kidnapping of her daughter by the shadowy force. She ran through the house and reclaimed her daughter at a time when the force was absent. The elderly people outside rejoiced and cheered the dreamer.

DREAM 10B—INTERPRETATION

The dreamer was in fact a bartender, who was addicted to multiple substances and was also addicted to gambling. Her mother was addicted to crack cocaine. The dreamer felt that her childhood was stolen from her. In spite of the addictions, both her mother and the dreamer were able to function and stay financially solvent, so that they were both "irresponsibly responsible." A house is the framework out of which one lives and can frequently represent the dreamer. The dream is saying that she is a complicated person who is frantically trying to satisfy the **Shadow** elements, the addictions. The effect of her **Shadow**, while she is consumed by her addictions, is to effectively remove both her own inner child and her four-year-old daughter from her.

The elderly crowd represented her inner emotionally supportive grandparents, who softened the effect of her own addicted and neglectful mother. The dreamer was reliving the dynamics of her childhood, as she was frequently emotionally unavailable to her daughter. The elderly grandparents, who were a significant part of her psyche, protested her ignoring her child. They rejoiced when she was able to reconnect with her daughter after she resisted her **Shadow** cravings.

DREAM 10C: THE SHADOW AS A LIFELONG STRUGGLE

An agoraphobic 17-year-old girl dreamt repeatedly that a dark, shadowy figure was holding a mirror up to her so that she could fully see herself.

DREAM 10C—INTERPRETATION

To get to know herself, she needed to look at her **Shadow**, which was a part of herself she needed to acknowledge so that she was less frightened by it. Repetitive or recurring dreams like this are frequently "big" dreams since the subconscious offers **Shadow** elements as a solution to similar conflicts in life. It behooves the dreamer to consider some elements of the **Shadow** to produce a satisfactory and wise solution. She did not want to acknowledge her dark **Shadow** side at all. She was consequently unable to benefit from some of the strength, the "get up and go," which is part of the **Shadow**. Rather than use the **Shadow** constructively, she refused to recognize that she had a dark side. Her fear of her own nature manifested symptomatically in agoraphobia and generalized anxiety.

Accepting their **Shadows** is especially difficult for well-behaved adolescents. I had a fifteen year old patient in therapy who was very suicidal. She attempted suicide three times. The last time, her family caught her getting ready to hang herself. In psychotherapy, she eventually revealed that she wanted to kill herself because she thought she was evil. She was having thoughts of murderous rage that were frustration with parents, siblings and friends. Her suicidal ideation was based on her idea that she was so uniquely evil that she had to kill herself before she hurt loved ones. She became less suicidal when she learned to release her anger assertively rather than castigating herself for being angry. She learned to accept her **Shadow's** cry for effective action.

The **Shadow** can frequently make people anxious. People with powerful **Shadows**, people with a lot of psychic energy, can be anxious that their **Shadow** will take control and they will do irreparable harm to significant others. A 28-year-old manager was in therapy to reduce her anxiety over fear that she would overuse her **Shadow** at work or in personal relationships. She wanted to appropriately calibrate her reaction to perceived violations of others so that her reaction to some degree matched the seriousness of the violation. She was tired of ruining relationships because she would often scorch the earth and take no prisoners on relatively minor issues. She ended up having resentful partners who felt they could not express disagreements to her. The other person typically left the relationship because he was sick of walking on eggshells to avoid her nuclear anger.

This therapist eventually believed what social psychology attribution theorists claimed. It seems that a person has a given level of emotional energy. Whether that energy is referred to as hate, love, fear, greed, or jealousy depends upon circumstances. Some people have a lot of energy and have large **Shadows**. These same people typically have a huge potential for good if they learn to channel their emotional energy positively. Conversely, people with large, positive, altruistic emotions have the potential for large **Shadows** if they choose to direct their emotional energy negatively. This is why there is nothing more evil than a good person gone bad, such as a cop becoming a gangster, and nothing as positive as a genocidal persecutor who reforms, such as Saint Paul.

DREAM 10D: EMOTIONAL ENERGY CONSERVATION

A 21-year-old coed dreamt that she was holding a baby girl. Across the road she saw a house burning. She did not know the couple that owned the house. She went to try to rescue people from the fire. A dark shadowy force tried to kill her when she was holding the baby while trying to look for the people she thought were in the fire. The shadowy figure finally forced her to leave the house.

DREAM 10D—INTERPRETATION

When she was five years old, her mother used her to listen to her mother's adult troubles with her husband. She acted as an adult child. She was very empathic to her mother's pain. Her mother was going through massive emotional changes at the time. The fire, which occurs at a house the dreamer does not own, signifies transformation or change, since fire changes matter into energy. Her **Shadow**, which obviously is the shadowy force, is trying to kill her, indicating that her old way of becoming too involved in others' emotional conflicts needed to change.

The part of her that risked her emotional safety needed to butt out of others' transformations, as people need to change primarily for themselves. She risked her tender emotions (represented by the baby girl she carried) too much for others. People need to be responsible for their own change. She could no longer risk her emotional health, especially for people that she did not really know.

CHAPTER 11:
CLEANING UP YOUR LIFE

Key 11: Bathrooms and showers are recurrent symbols because they point to what the person wants to eliminate or clean up in his or her life.

We call it "elimination" for the reason that the body is getting rid of waste it no longer needs, and which can be toxic, if retained. Similarly, the bathroom is a place where metaphorical cleansing of emotions takes places. The toilet is used to rid oneself of toxic emotions, while the shower/bathtub is a place to cleanse oneself of the residue of negative experiences. After being raped, the first thing the victim wants to do is take a shower to cleanse herself of the traumatic experience.

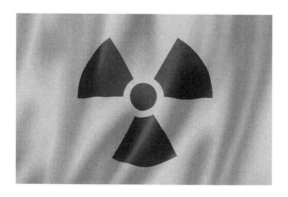

Dreams use the bathroom and showers metaphorically to indicate what the dreamer needs to get rid of in his or her life to fully integrate. The goal of mental health, as Dr. Carl Jung pointed out, is for the dreamer to fully integrate all the masculine (action) parts of the psyche with all the feminine (emotion) parts of the psyche. This is, of course, important, regardless of the gender of the dreamer. An important part of that integration is to discard or trim unneeded and potentially toxic parts of the psyche.

The dream frequently explicates what needs to be terminated in the dreamer's life by the material that immediately precedes going to the bathroom in the dream. Having an argument with someone and then going to the bathroom to urinate is usually indicative of needing to get rid of toxic emotion (urine is toxic water and water almost invariably is emotion in dreams). Feces is even stronger and is usually making a more general statement to the effect of "you need to get this stuff (euphemism) out of your life."

Doing laundry or references to laundry can similarly point to the need to clean up your defenses, since clothes almost always represent our defenses, i.e., they are the front we present to the world, which often say much about us.

In any case, the bathroom is metaphorically an internal source of water that is used to cleanse or eliminate negative emotions. The healing powers of water have long been recognized. New souls are baptized in water. The practices of lying in healing waters or swimming in the spiritual healing waters of the Ganges River in India point to the curative powers of calming and cleansing emotions.

DREAM 11A: WHEN YOU GOTTA GO

A 38-year-old woman dreamt that there was a black girl sitting on a toilet, carefully measuring how much urine she was allowed to pass, which the woman knew was a minute amount. The dreamer thought she should have been catheterized so that all the urine could be removed completely and properly.

DREAM 11A—INTERPRETATION

Water invariably represents emotions. Female figures usually deal with emotions. The darker the skin, the more soul is being called for (we even call it soul music). In dreams, bathrooms represent the place where we want to rid ourselves of things that we no longer use, need, or are toxic to us. The dreamer was very conflicted over expressing anger to her husband. The careful measurement of urine emitted represented her excessive efforts to avoid letting too much anger out. She frequently hid her anger or reduced it to the point that her husband was unable to understand her. Her soul or subconscious was recommending that she fully and appropriately express toxic emotion. It was recommending that she completely remove the anger from her system, even if she had to go to extraordinary efforts (catheterize) to do so.

DREAM 11B: LETTING GO OF TOXIC EMOTION

A 34-year-old woman dreamt that she was sitting on a toilet in the middle of a shopping mall. There were no walls or partitions around the toilet. She could be seen by everyone. She felt exposed and vulnerable. No one passing by even looked in her direction. Everyone acted completely disinterested.

DREAM 11B—INTERPRETATION

Dreams frequently give information or set the stage concerning the main theme of the dream via the opening setting. Shopping malls typically indicate that the dream is going to talk about how the dreamer was "mauled" either physically or psychologically in life. That it occurred in a commercial establishment indicated that it was going to talk about how the mistreatment affected her work or business life. The toilet indicated that she had psychic contents and emotions that needed to be washed from her system. The lack of walls indicated how exposed and vulnerable she felt about the emotional scars.

The curious point of this dream was that no passerby looked at her or cared. On the intrapsychic level, each passerby is a part of her psyche. (This view *agrees* completely with the movie *Inception*. This movie emphasized that all the characters in a dream are projections of the dreamer's subconscious.) The dream was trying to reassure her that she rose above the hurts to some degree; however, it also pointed to her ignoring working on these scars by, for example, not attending therapy. She was the oldest and parentified child who took care of her siblings in an extremely dysfunctional family.

On the interpersonal level, she was well regarded at work, which she could scarcely believe because the transference from the past was so strong. Significantly, she was severely neglected by her parents and devoted nearly all of her emotional energy to taking care of others. This pattern had continued into her present work life (which employers, of course, loved.)

DREAM 11C: LESBIAN PHOBIA

A 20-year-old attractive woman dreamt that she lived in a large and spacious richly adorned mansion. She was in a classic-appearing sumptuous courtyard. She was being followed by her mother, a beautiful woman and eight gay male servants. She was approached by the beautiful woman, but decided she had to go into a large bathroom.

She was followed by the beautiful woman, her mother and the eight gay male servants. She was in a stall going to the bathroom. Much to her annoyance, the beautiful woman kept opening the door to the stall. The dreamer was always able to close the door successfully.

DREAM 11C—INTERPRETATION

A house can represent the dreamer since it is the framework out of which one lives. The dream was recognizing that she was a complex and attractive woman with many intellectual achievements by using an extravagant mansion as the setting for the dream. The beautiful woman represented the part of her worry that was recently attracted to a pretty friend. The servants were the larger part of herself that liked men. It was her experience that men most often tried to help her and frequently became servile to her because of their attraction to her. Her mother in the dream was her mother introject, which indicated that her superego was involved since the dream was addressing matters of conscience. Parental figures in dreams frequently signal that matters involving what we were taught to believe as children are involved.

That she went to the bathroom indicated that she was trying to get rid of something that was bothering or annoying her. The beautiful woman that kept opening the stall door and the dreamer closing the door indicated how uncomfortable she was with the idea that she felt momentarily attracted to her good friend, which was something she would never take action on. The dream tried to reassure her with the eight gay men that the part of herself that likes men is stronger and more predominant.

DREAM 11D: ALMOST BLOWING A GASKET

A 32-year-old woman dreamt that she was a passenger in a car her husband was driving. She was concerned with whether he took care of the car properly. Specifically, she thought that he didn't check the engine fluids. The car started to overheat, which was due to the lack of fluids. She wanted him to stop, but he insisted that they continue to a gas station. She was angry when they arrived at the gas station. She used the restroom there. When she came out, she was angry that her husband was giving marijuana away free to a crowd of bystanders.

DREAM 11D—INTERPRETATION

Interpreting the dream at the first level, each character in the dream is considered to be a part of her psyche. Women usually go more with emotion and men usually go more with action in most dreams. A car is how one gets somewhere in life. She was angry over the action part of her psyche not considering her emotions enough (not supplying fluids, which are usually emotions), to the point that it endangered her progress in life. Her going to a gas station and using the restroom indicated that she needed to recharge her energy (refuel the car) and get rid of toxic emotions, as restrooms are the repository for eliminating waste. The dream ends with her being dissatisfied with the action part of herself, her husband, drugging the rest of her psyche into oblivion.

On the interpersonal level, she was very unhappy with her husband losing a contract due to his playing golf too much. She was working way too many hours and was ignoring her emotional needs, as was her husband. Rather than dealing with these problems directly, she was isolating herself in the evening and smoking marijuana.

DREAM 11E: HANDLING EMOTIONS IN A RELATIONSHIP

A 54-year-old executive was having marital problems. He dreamt that his wife was swimming in their pool at home. When she got out of the pool, her two small children ran after her with determination. She ran into the bathroom and urinated.

DREAM 11E—INTERPRETATION

He worked long hours, they had two toddler boys, and his wife complained that he was not emotionally supportive. A swimming pool contains water, which is emotion. Specifically, a pool represents the emotions or emotional atmosphere at home. The two toddler boys are emphasizing his dependence on his wife to navigate emotions. He typically came home and complained about work for long periods of time. In his dream, his wife represented his emotions. In dreams and life, a bathroom is where one gets rid of toxic emotions. The advice of the dream was that he needed to be less involved with toxic dependence and emotional whining, which was why his wife was urinating (eliminating excessive toxic water or emotion).

This dream is a condensation of intrapsychic and interpersonal processes. Described above is the intrapsychic view, which is more difficult, but frequently more helpful. Intrapsychic interpretation is the first level of dream interpretation, where one considers each character or animal to be part of the dreamer's psyche. Intrapsychic interpretation accuracy can be as high as eighty to ninety percent.

If interpreted interpersonally, the level of accurate interpretation frequently drops to fifty percent or less unless the interpreter knows the dreamer extremely well and understands unconscious forces. At the interpersonal level, the dream is recommending that he be more supportive in helping with the emotional demands of the children when she is in need of some alone time.

Key 11 Addendum: Cleaning house often refers to cleaning one's life up, either emotionally or physically. Washing or cleaning clothes refers specifically to modifying one's defenses. Closets in dreams are frequently reservoirs of family secrets.

DREAM 11F: CLEANING UP YOUR LIFE AND DE-FENSES

A 42-year-old woman with medical problems dreamt that she was talking to a female professional cleaner. The cleaner brought a friend of the dreamer along with her to help her clean. The dreamer was upset that she previously was not told by cleaner that the dreamer's friend would be helping. The dreamer was offended by her friend coming to the house uninvited. The dreamer was worried that she had to arrange items in the house so that the cleaners could clean. She wanted to hide many items. The dreamer saw herself furiously stashing many items throughout the house, especially behind the television. She also thought she had better do her laundry, because she was embarrassed and she did not trust the cleaners not to damage her clothes. Things that were permanently stained were hidden in a closet.

Dream 11F—Interpretation

A house represents the framework out of which we live. As such, it can sometimes represent the body. This dream is a condensation that could be interpreted emotionally and physically. Emotionally, she had been in therapy for four sessions with the stated goal that she wanted to clean up her life, i.e., "clean house." She talked to a professional, this therapist, whom she regarded as a "mental cleaner." It is very important to listen to the language and common sayings in a dream and then expand upon the metaphors evoked.

She realized that the therapist allied with a friendly and less defensive part of her subconscious to put her house, i.e., her life, in order. Her response was that her resistance was somewhat mobilized. She did not want therapist to know every detail of her life, symbolized by her stashing items about the house. She literally did not want her therapy to get as personal as it needed to get to change long-standing emotional patterns.

It is interesting that the dream took special notice of her hiding items behind the television. Television is a mass communication device that informs the world. She did not want her faults broadcast to the world.

Her doing the laundry indicated she was embarrassed by some of her defenses and for now was leery of the therapist changing her habitual defensiveness. New clients are frequently unsure about how much "dirty laundry" they can reveal to a therapist. The most important family secrets are stored in a closet, as she was not ready to reveal the most traumatic abuse she had suffered as a child, which came out in later sessions and was truly horrendous.

It is speculative, but intriguing to consider in light of her medical problems, that this dream may be a condensation that addresses her physical health as well. She may want a doctor to help her heal physically, but may fear that additional physical ailments may be revealed. We frequently avoid being made aware of what we subconsciously suspect.

CHAPTER 12:
ARCHETYPES

"I am taking this time to create my day. I am infecting the Quantum Field. If there is a spiritual aspect to myself, and the observer's watching me the whole time that I am doing this, then show me a sign today that you paid attention to any one of these things that I created. Bring them in a way I won't expect so that I'm surprised at my ability to be able to experience these things, and make it so that I have no doubt that it came from you."

Dr. Joe Dispensary, What the Bleep Do We Know, 2004

The above prayer can be used to invoke the energies of your dominant Archetype.

Key 12: Archetypes are ingrained in all human consciousness. The human race at one time was a single tribe that spread to the corners of the earth carrying these fundamental images and associated patterns of thought that comprise the different archetypes. The world is composed of consciousness, which chooses which archetype to emphasize in a given life circumstance. These conscious choices are made under the pervasive influence of the subconscious, which is where the fundamental archetypes are stored by the individual under the influence of culture and quantum consciousness effects. Archetypes are an inherent part of all cultures. Culture and the quantum communicating effects of consciousness propel the transmission of archetypes through the ages. Archetypes provide a special energy that produces numinous experiences, which are glimpses of the sacred, divine and/or transcendental states. Numinous was a concept Dr. Jung used which originated with Rudolf Otto. The numinous experience is transcendent and

sacred, simultaneously evoking fascination, wonder and awe in the viewer. Numinous archetypal experiences bring luminosity, or light, to the person.

Archetypal experiences and the associated energy are beyond words. If one can tie into their own particular dominant archetype, it energizes one's most important endeavors.

There are basic patterns of thought transmitted to individuals through culture, which are called archetypes. There are new paradigms indicating that the world and universe are composed of consciousness and its effects (Amit Goswami in the documentary "The Quantum Activist," circa 2010). One can view these archetypes as thought patterns embedded in consciousness. Beyond the strange quantum events where the seemingly impossible occurs, at a practical level these thought patterns are handed down through the ages by culture.

Archetypes reside in a culture and are vital to what Carl Jung called the collective unconscious. Cultural remnants involving classical architecture, religious figures, Greek gods, pop culture icons and historical figures are some signs that archetypal patterns

of thought are at play in the individual's subconscious. Knowledge of basic archetypes is fundamental to dream interpretation. The **Shadow Archetype** discussed previously is the most important archetype in the process of change.

DREAM 12A: HOLY ARCHETYPE

A 27-year-old man saw himself in a dream climbing a high and rugged mountain with caves in it. He next saw the Roman Coliseum, with a huge pillar in the middle. On top of the pillar was the Holy Grail. Four men were on fire and they were trying to tip the pillar toward them so that they could receive the healing waters of the Holy Grail. He next saw himself in his kitchen with a small boxing ring inside the kitchen. Inside the boxing ring was a miniaturized fighter that looked exactly like himself. He was fighting a comparatively huge black man. The dreamer thought that he won the boxing match.

DREAM 12A—INTERPRETATION

On the Thematic Apperception Test (TAT), a projective personality test that reveals subconscious motivations by the stories a test taker tells while viewing works of art, a story about someone climbing mountains is considered to be revealing an underlying high need for achievement. Caves, because they go beyond what one can see on the surface, are usually entrances to the unconscious. This part of the dream is predicting that it is going to be a difficult task that will require him to consult with his emotions as he works on the task.

The Roman Coliseum is a classic archetypal image. When one sees Greek columns, Roman architecture, Egyptian pyramids, or ashrams in India, one is virtually always dealing with archetypal elements, as these cultures are the basis of modern civilizations. The Roman pillar in the middle of the Coliseum and the Holy Grail were archetypal to the extreme. The quest for the Holy Grail preoccupied medieval European cultures. It is a circular object at the top and harkens back spiritually to Jesus Christ's last supper, where he had Communion with his disciples. The quest for the Holy Grail is Man's search for his soul.

The four men who are on fire represented constructive change of actions. Men tend to go with action parts of the psyche. Four is a number of stability, as there are four directions, four seasons, four legs to a table and chair, etc. Fire virtually always represents change. He was taking constructive action to heal his soul. He was trying to heal and save his psyche/soul.

The kitchen is a place of creativity. The miniaturized boxing ring represented the place where the dreamer was trying to conquer his conflicts. The darker the skin (the opposing boxer), the more soul is being called for. The dream predicted that he would encounter much conflict that required him to deal with his soul/conscience. The dream projected that he was going through an arduous journey and fighting with matters of conscience. The dream was about his conflicts about starting a business with a friend that included a casino.

We cause the most extensive changes in our character and in our functioning by reprioritizing archetypes within ourselves. There may be archetypes within us that are used excessively. At the same time, there may be parts unknown to ourselves because we imprisoned these archetypes in the **Shadow**. Virtually every part of our personality can be used for good in some situation in life. Having access to all parts of our personality promotes adaptability and versatility and improves personal functioning. Let us look at some archetypes the author found to be especially helpful in psychotherapy.

CHAPTER 13:
THE SHADOW ARCHETYPE

Key 13: The Shadow is focused upon the dreamer and will often dramatically use aggressive instincts to protect the dreamer.

Using the **Shadow in service to the ego** is simply using aggressive and unwanted parts of ourselves to accomplish positive goals. Every archetype has **Shadow** aspects. The **Warrior Archetype is Shadow related**. The **Warrior Archetype** most notably relies on combat, when it is used properly, for the protection of society and the promotion of shared goals. Sports, business and even educational competition use energy from the **Shadow** to accomplish goals. The **Shadow** can be used for positive purposes when it is in contact with other parts of the subconscious that put limits on the **Shadow's** behavior. The **Shadow** gives us the "get up and go," while other archetypes put limits on the **Shadow**, so that its energy is used for positive goals. An unbridled **Shadow** produces an angry and/or irresponsible character, i.e., a sociopath.

The **Shadow** is only dangerous when other structures are not available to positively direct its behavior. If one is not in contact at all with the **Shadow**, there is danger that it may become frustrated and take over the personality because the rest of the person is not considering the **Shadow's** input. When you have had it up to your ears in frustration, the **Shadow** will remove you from the situation by whatever means are available. This accounts for the situations where the person did something in her own interest in such a dramatic way that she later could hardly believe she did it. The **Shadow** is protective and focuses on self-survival.

DREAM 13A: HAVING A TALK WITH GODZILLA

A 19-year-old college student dreamt that he watched Godzilla lumber through his hometown, leaving a trail of destruction. Godzilla at one point picked up a little boy and smashed him to the ground before trampling him underneath as he continued his destructive binge. The dream then shifted to his home, where a human-sized Godzilla was sitting on the couch with him. This humanized Godzilla asked the dreamer, "Do you think your girlfriend is the best thing for you or could you do better?"

DREAM 13A—INTERPRETATION

He had a girlfriend that he loved but was increasingly alarmed and worried about her drinking increasing after the death of her alcoholic father. He felt hurt that she was ignoring his feelings as she was caught up in grieving for her functioning alcoholic father, who helped her financially. He felt in many ways that she left the relationship emotionally and he was angry.

Godzilla represented the aggressive animal instincts within him that he knew were destructive because they were killing the little boy feelings within him. When he tried to be reasonable with his id or instinctive reactions (the human-sized Godzilla), he was wondering if he should get out of the relationship. Being ignored by his girlfriend ignited transference because he was ignored by his family as a child.

Transference simply means that emotion from a past situation is amplifying the emotion in a current conflict. Transference magnifies the emotions involved in the current situation. Transference may make a person three times angrier than he would be otherwise. The transference-related anger released the gigantic Godzilla rather than a human-sized and more humane Godzilla. Godzilla was the **Shadow** side of his instincts. As Freud noted, two of the main instincts are sex and aggression.

The human-sized Godzilla was poignant symbolism of his **Shadow** trying to reason with him. The **Shadow** was urging him to be reasonable and protect himself by getting away from the girlfriend. The **Shadow** was well aware of the destructive anger and aggression ignited within the dreamer by his transference of the apathetic family attitude to the uncaring girlfriend.

DREAM 13B: WILD THING

A 32-year-old woman dreamt that she was driving a car with her black, "jailbreak," wild ex-convict. They went to a female professor's house who at the time was her main advisor. Inside the house, the professor acted motherly toward the dreamer. There was also another intelligent female friend there who took many of the same college courses. She left the wild boyfriend in the car. She suddenly realized she needed to look out the front door to see if the boyfriend stole the car. She quickly opened the door a crack to check and she woke up at that moment.

DREAM 13B—INTERPRETATION

A car in a dream represents modern progress through life. The dreamer had an active sex life that worried her. The wild illicit boyfriend represented **Shadow** sexual actions (since the passenger is a male) of sexual adventuring. The professor represented a condensation of the **Mother Archetype** and the **Wise Woman**. Her smart co-ed friend was there to emphasize the need for her to use her intellect to temper her emotions (especially since all characters in the house were female). A house frequently represents the dreamer in some sense, since it is the framework out of which one lives. The dream was literally advising her to monitor her tendency to be sexually adventurous because major damage could occur.

The danger was that her ability to progress in life (the car) could be stolen by her dangerous behavior (the **Shadow** wild boyfriend.) She let that part of herself out of prison because it was previously totally suppressed. Given the course of the dream, it may be a wise idea to put that portion of her personality on parole for a while.

Chapter 14:
The Trickster Archetype

Key 14: The role of the Trickster is to help us endure difficult situations. The Trickster typically bends or breaks the rules so that the individual or organization can function. Following the formal rules is often unnecessarily burdensome, if not making accomplishing real productive work impossible. The Trickster typically makes the best of a bad situation.

The Trickster is related to the **Shadow Archetype**. Like the **Shadow Archetype**, it is not there merely to make life difficult. There is real purpose to the **Trickster's** ways. Like the frustrated **Shadow**, it ultimately will force the issue if it must in order to motivate the dreamer to take the necessary steps to create the best possible solution for the dreamer. The **Shadow** directly confronts the issue in situations where that is possible in order to get the dreamer to take actions that will be protective for the dreamer in the long run. The **Trickster** gets the dreamer to momentarily withhold judgment to use manipulative means because the dreamer's very survival may be in danger. The **Trickster's** specialty is making impossible situations somehow work for the benefit of the dreamer.

A great story illustrating the value of the **Trickster** took place during the Spanish Inquisition. At that time, rabbis were burned at the stake. The Inquisitors gave the rabbis a chance to avoid being burned at the stake. The idea was that if the rabbi was given a chance and the results confirmed that he should be burned at the stake, there would be less guilt because the will of God was supposedly involved in the decision.

The rabbi to be burned was told that the Inquisitor was holding two pieces of paper in his hands. If the rabbi chose the hand which was holding a sheet of paper saying "yes" on it, the rabbi would be burned at the stake. If he chose the hand with the paper that said "no" on it, his life would be spared.

The rabbi immediately grabbed the paper out of one of the Inquisitor's hands, placed it in his mouth, and swallowed it. The rabbi told the Inquisitor that since it was known that one paper said "yes" while the other said "no," the answer he chose would be the opposite of that remaining on the other piece of paper. When they looked at the remaining sheet of paper, it said "yes," that he should be burned at the stake. Therefore, it was reasoned that the sheet the rabbi swallowed must have said "no" to his being burned at the stake and his life was spared.

The rabbi knew that he had to eat one of the sheets of paper. Why? Because the rabbi knew that both pieces of paper said "yes," that he should be burned at the stake. The **Trickster** saved the rabbi's life by recognizing that it was an impossible situation that required counter-manipulation, which is the **Trickster's** specialty.

DREAM 14A: THE TRICKSTER MAKES THE SITUATION WORK

A 33-year-old woman dreamt of many people jumping off a cliff. One man did a back flip and plunged into the shallow end of the water below. He died on impact. The rest of the jumpers fell into somewhat deeper water and survived because they did not do risky back flips. The dreamer saw herself making out with her previous boss. Her boss was a manipulative wheeler-dealer type. Her benevolent father watched the passion approvingly. The crazy, witch wife of her boss tried to break them up.

DREAM 14A—INTERPRETATION

The dreamer was a heavy abuser of LSD and other serious hallucinogenic drugs. She stopped after going through a drug abuse rehabilitation program approximately five years earlier. The many people jumping off the cliff were the many different aspects of her subconscious involved in serious drug abuse. They dove into the ocean, which is the primordial symbol of the subconscious and emotion. Their risky, high flying behavior is cushioned and mitigated by the ocean so that they survived, with the exception of the highest risk taker, the back flipper. His actions led to his death because he was the shallowest emotionally. The dreamer's most risky behavior or actions (typically action parts of the subconscious are presented as male) died or stopped in drug rehab. The death of a character in a dream many times indicates that the part of the unconscious that the character represents needs to "die" or radically change, i.e., that the person needs to drastically change that part of themselves.

The making out scene represents her emotions integrating with her inner **Trickster** (an action archetype seen as male). Sexual activity in dreams is often a major indicator of integration because the male part of the dreamer (the dreamer's actions) are integrating with the female part of the dreamer (the dreamer's emotions). Each major character in a dream represents part of the dreamer's subconscious at the first level of interpretation. Archetypes are patterns of thought handed down through the ages through culture. When there is no way a situation can work out if only the formal rules are followed, the **Trickster** makes it happen through his manipulations. The dreamer's inner negative witch mother introject was incensed that she was integrating with the **Trickster** and tried to stop it from happening. Her positive, action-oriented father introject viewed the integration positively. He knew that it would help her actions adapt to the business situation.

In her life, she recently had to change her work practices at an employment agency because it was not possible to do the job in the manner she had meticulously approached her work in the past. She found that she had to adopt some of her previous supervisor's ways of doing things. None of the practices were illegal, but she was having trouble with the situational business ethics that were used. The dream was reassuring her about using her inner **Trickster** to accomplish a job that really could not be done otherwise. The dream tried to give her permission to accomplish what she needed to do.

DREAM 14B: SELLING OUT IS OVER

A 36-year-old man dreamt that he and a beautiful woman companion were exiled to Eastern Europe, which was impoverished and drab. They were supposed to go to a circus and give a receipt to the wheeler-dealer manager. They discovered the receipt verified they had been sold into slavery. The woman shot and killed the wheeler-dealer manager, who immediately was transformed into a kind and gentle male supervisor the dreamer had worked for some years before. The dream shifted to his being allowed to return to America. He was transported to another scene where he was talking to an empathic woman while they were eating giant prawns.

Dream 14B—Interpretation

Each character in the dream represented a part of his psyche. The initial action tells us (by the presence of the beautiful female **Anima**) that the dream is going to be describing what happened to him emotionally. He was addicted to opiates until recently. He was a slave to the drug and lived in shambles (thus he was sold into slavery in drab Eastern Europe). The wheeler-dealer manager represented the dark side of his inner **Trickster**, as he was running a three-ring circus while selling his positive emotions, the beautiful woman, into slavery.

When someone dies in a dream, it usually means that there is a part of the dreamer's psyche that needs to die, that the dreamer should quit relying upon that part of his mind for now. The dream was stating in the strongest manner possible that he needed to use his emotions to rid himself of his slavery to drugs. The commerce and the reselling of drugs were making a circus of his life. His positive emotions, the beautiful woman, needed to shoot a **Shadow Trickster**, which was serving an addiction rather than the dreamer.

The dream indicated that he needed to use the action part of himself that was like a previous supervisor (which was the **Wise Old Man Archetype**). His life dramatically improved as a result of following this mentor (he came home to America). Prawns are nourishment from the ocean, which is the most significant symbol of subconscious emotion there is. His feeding upon the contents of his subconscious with an empathic emotional listener was a recommendation to attend therapy.

Dream 14C: Use the Wheeler Dealer (Trickster) Part of Yourself

A 48-year-old woman dreamt that she saw a former boyfriend staring at her like he knew what she was all about and could discern her motives to his own advantage.

DREAM 14C—INTERPRETATION

This dream fragment is being presented to illustrate that, with a knowledge of Jungian archetypes, one can say a lot about a strong image. The particular boyfriend she remembered was an extremely manipulative man who nearly always received what he wanted. He was very successful financially and started many thriving businesses.

Her subconscious was trying to get her to look at, and use, to some degree, her inner **Trickster**. She was trying to start a business and was becoming frustrated with the necessary maneuvers and presentation needed to ensure the success of the business. The **Trickster** is a wheeler-dealer carnival barker who makes his business look as attractive as possible so that others cooperate. The **Trickster**, in its most extreme form, can be psychopathic if the person did not develop the other parts of the psyche enough, so that the **Trickster's** behavior becomes out of bounds and over the top. This woman was very moral and conscientious to the point that she did not use the **Trickster** enough to succeed in business.

DREAM 14D: FEELING LIKE I WON THE LOTTERY

A 42-year-old woman dreamt that she got rid of an undermining colleague at work by outmaneuvering her politically. The other woman was assigned to a different division in the company. The scene then shifted to the dreamer winning the lottery.

DREAM 14D—INTERPRETATION

If you look at each character as being a part of the dreamer's own psyche, intrapsychically the dream is saying that she got rid of or reduced a manipulative (**Trickster Archetype**) part of herself. In a dream, money is energy. She felt relief and freedom from social tension after the woman was reassigned. The renewed energy she felt, symbolized by winning the lottery in the dream, was palpable.

At the second and interpersonal level, she did have a recent competition at work where an undermining colleague lost. Nearly simultaneously, she won six thousand dollars in a lottery. Jung called such meaningful coincidences "synchronicity." Synchronicity occurs when two unrelated events happen in such a way that they seem related. Like the Chinese, Carl Jung believed that synchronicity in one's life frequently had meaning and one ignored it at one's own peril. Money is certainly energy at the intrapsychic level. At the interpersonal level, money is sometimes just...ah...money. As Freud said, sometimes a cigar is just a cigar.

CHAPTER 15:
THE HEROIC MASCULINE ARCHETYPE

Key 15: The Heroic Masculine is vital to making progress in life, as this part of the psyche promotes, protects and encourages the dreamer to take positive action.

The **Heroic Masculine Archetype** is the most positive part of masculinity (or the action part of the psyche, whether the dreamer is male or female). Its model is "to serve and protect" and that is what it does for a healthy person. On the interpersonal level, this is a part of the person that would literally die to protect loved ones. Good soldiers and high-functioning policemen have a strong dose of the **Heroic Masculine** in their psyches.

The counterbalance to the **Heroic Masculine** is the **Savage Masculine**. The **Savage Masculine** performs **Shadow** functions of protecting the person in dire circumstances and is willing to do whatever needs to be done to defend the person. The **Savage Masculine** is easily recognizable by its drastic actions in do-or-die circumstances. The **Heroic Masculine** is central to people getting better in psychotherapy. At some point, the insights gained in psychotherapy of specific positive actions which need to be taken are fulfilled by the **Heroic Masculine's** insistence upon performing actions that are in the best interests of the person.

The **Heroic Masculine** is often "tall, dark and handsome." In fairy tales and myths, he is the knight on the white horse or the one defending another person's honor. He helps the person be assertive in taking actions to promote the person and those close to him or her.

It is the **Heroic Masculine**, as will be discussed later, who has any chance at all of standing up successfully to the **Shadow** side of the **Queen**. As we shall see, the **Shadow** side of the **Queen** can equal the destructiveness of the **Savage Masculine**. The **Savage Masculine** tends to engage in destructive action, while the **Shadow** side of the **Queen** is all about power and wielding control over others. It is often the effects of these archetypes that manifest in post-traumatic stress that has to be dealt with in psychotherapy. The **Heroic Masculine** is usually the long-awaited rescuer.

DREAM 15A: THINK OF THE RIGHT ACTION

A 22-year-old man dreamt that he was a commander in the army, in charge of a platoon. The men in his platoon were being shot in the head one by one. The commander (himself) was chasing a naked woman instead of focusing on his men.

DREAM 15A—INTERPRETATION

An army commander is the representation of the **Heroic Masculine** because he literally is willing to die for others, as good soldiers are. Masculine entities typically represent parts of the dreamer's psyche that are concerned with the dreamer's actions. The naked woman in a dream can often represent the dreamer's exposed and vulnerable emotions. His subconscious was pointing out that instead of focusing on what he had to do, he was focusing on his emotions too much and was losing initiative. The dream was saying that his focusing on his emotions too much was endangering the action parts of his psyche. In this case, the client was so focused on depression that he could hardly accomplish anything.

DREAM 15B: YOU MAKE ME FEEL LIKE A NATURAL WOMAN

A 24-year-old woman dreamt that she was swimming near an island. On the island were her father and her boyfriend. Both her father and her boyfriend were very protective and epitomized what is meant by the **Heroic Masculine**. When she was swimming, two killer whales appeared. She swam back to the island where her father, her boyfriend and a little girl with blond hair and blue eyes reassured her. She swam back out away from the island and five happy dolphins swam out near her.

DREAM 15B—INTERPRETATION

Aquatic creatures inhabiting the water represent having energy in your subconscious emotions. When the two killer whales appeared, they represented deep unconscious anger, which frightened her. She returned to what for her was a psychological sanctuary, the island that contained her father and boyfriend. She received reassurance from her father introject and her inner **Heroic Masculine**, represented by her protective boyfriend. The little girl on the island represented the **Divine Child Archetype**, which symbolizes the hopes and dreams the dreamer has for the future (in my experience, in United States Caucasian culture, the **Divine Child** frequently has blue eyes and blond hair and often is a little girl roughly age five to 10.) The dolphins represented her positive validating energy, which was the result of much work in group therapy. This dream celebrated her progress in feeling more secure and able to face challenges.

CHAPTER 16:
THE QUEEN ARCHETYPE
(LONG LIVE THE QUEEN!)

Key 16: The Shadow Queen represents negative emotionality and typically is domineering, controlling and capricious.

The **Queen** is a strong archetype. The positive **Queen** is regal fortitude and perseverance powerful enough to lead a nation successfully. It is important to recognize this positive aspect, but it seldom shows up in dreams because this portion of the **Queen** is not a problem. People seldom come into therapy because they feel too regal and powerful. It is the **Shadow Queen**, which is negative, domineering and manipulative emotionality that presents problems for the dreamer. When I talk about the **Queen** in this book, I will usually be talking about the **Shadow Queen**.

Just as men need the **Savage Masculine** to defend themselves in war and combat, women need the **Queen** to defend themselves when protection by other means is not available. The **Queen** is likely to become a greater factor when a woman feels backed into a corner with no allies. In a confrontation between the **Queen** and the **Savage Masculine**, if they are given equal technology, my money is on the **Queen**.

For example, in roller derby it is predictable that the men will engage in a certain amount of fighting and dirty dealings, but there are some lines of behavior they will not cross. When women play roller derby, there are no lines. Anything can and does happen. The **Queen** is ruthless and usually only engages an opponent when it is highly probable that she will win. The positive **Queen**, for which I will give an example at the end of this chapter, is a nurturing source of persevering guidance.

The sheer psychological power of the **Queen** was honored in history despite cultural prejudices. For example, in the 1800s, when women were severely repressed, Queen Victoria ruled England and its Commonwealth at the height of this empire's strength. Joan of Arc was a French military leader who was legendary. Even in Russia's history, Catherine the Great was a force enshrined with title and national commitment. Even though previous cultures were highly prejudiced toward and oppressed women, these barriers melted away when cultures recognized the awesome psychological power of the **Queen**.

The more the importance of physical strength fades, the greater the influence of the **Queen** will be as technology severely reduces society's reliance upon physical force and power. It does not take much physical strength to launch a missile.

DREAM 16A: BREAKING THE CHAINS THAT BIND ME

A 28-year-old man dreamt that he was a knight who was trying to kill a medieval queen. The scene suddenly shifted to a kitchen, where the queen had the knight bound in chains. Through sheer force of will, the knight was able to break out of the chains as blood flew through the air. A princess entered the scene and proceeded to successfully resolve their differences, so that the queen and knight were at peace with one another.

DREAM 16A—INTERPRETATION

The first thing to notice is the medieval royalty aspect to this dream. This is an archetypal dream employing images common in and well known to Western culture. Archetypal dreams are usually "big" dreams that are important to the dreamer and hit on age old conflicts that man has been trying to figure out for millennia. A knight is representative of the **Heroic Masculine**, with an emphasis on chivalrous actions. The queen in this dream was a **Shadow Queen** and represented negative emotionality. The **Queen** in such situations is typically domineering and controlling.

The **Shadow Queen** is disruptive to the **Heroic Masculine** and interferes with the accomplishment of positive goals.

The kitchen is a place of creativity, since nurturing and pleasing sustenance is created there. The knight breaking out of the chains was symbolic of the dreamer breaking free of negative and controlling emotionality, which was stunting his creativity. Blood is red and relates to love and anger, depending upon the context. The blood flying through the air indicated that he was freeing his passion and the right to express his anger.

The dreamer was an art student who was having trouble expressing his creativity. He was too strict and stern in his business dealings with an art institute, which was an effect of the negative **Queen** portion of his psyche. The princess portion of his psyche, whom you can think of as a positive Queen-to-be, had positive emotions of appropriate assertiveness and openness, which reconciled his rigidity so that he could be more creative.

DREAM 16B: THE NEGATIVE QUEEN ATTACKS

A 29-year-old man dreamt that he was in a healing facility with Greek architecture. A beautiful woman was on a gurney. She was being attacked by an older female dressed in black.

DREAM 16B—INTERPRETATION

The Greek architecture was a sign that here were ancient cultural or archetypal thought patterns in play. They were in a place of healing (this client was in therapy for three months at this point). The beautiful woman on the gurney was an **Anima**, or ideal woman, who represented the new and positive emotional attitudes that he was developing. He was starting to view himself as being more capable of achievement. The older woman in black was the negative mother introject (or **Shadow Queen**) within the dreamer, which was fighting him and trying to distort his new attitudes.

Both of the dream figures are females, indicating that there was an emotional war going on. The **Shadow Queen** is totally controlling, domineering, capricious and malevolent.

Such a **Queen's** attitude is Ask not what I can do for you, ask what you have done for me lately. The dark **Shadow Queen** casts aspersions on self-improvement. This part of the psyche's attitude toward self-improvement is, "Who do you think you are?" In spite of her negative connotations, it needs to be recognized that, if not taken to an extreme, which is often the case in psychotherapy, her skepticism can be a necessary counterbalance to prideful heroic action.

DREAM 16C: THAT LITTLE BOY OF MINE

A 34-year-old woman dreamt that she was Snow White. She was taking a little boy, the "Little Prince," to a play. There was a parallel evil and dark Snow White who hovered ominously around them, so that the dreamer felt she was protecting the eight-year-old boy. She entered an area that resembled a combination of Sea World and an amusement park. She was carrying the now rather heavy boy everywhere they went. She finally obtained some relief from the burden by going down a fun water slide with the little boy.

She then decided to take him to the "Lost and Found" at a hotel because she somehow knew that some parents were there. The parents refused to take the child and told her that she should take the little boy home with her. She took the little boy home and her parents greeted her at the door.

DREAM 16C—INTERPRETATION

The dream began by recognizing her idealized image of a woman, Snow White. Snow White is an extremely positive **Anima**, or idealized woman. The "evil" Snow White is her feminine **Shadow**, which contains elements of the **Shadow Queen**. The little boy was an idealized (the Little Prince) action part of herself that she was trying to develop. Over and over, the dream recommended that she engage in "play" (she said the word repeatedly when referring to the theatrical production) to learn how to properly manage that part of her. Specifically, the dream indicated that play would teach her how to be less overprotective and cautious regarding her action self. Play (going down the water slide in an amusement park) allowed her to be close to the action part of herself with a minimum of emotional conflict.

The dream emphasized that she was carrying too much of the burden of life with her emotions (which was the reason the boy became heavier to the woman who was transporting him). She was uncomfortable integrating with an action part of herself and at one point wanted to give it away (to parental figures at the "Lost and Found" at a commercial establishment). The dream appeared to be saying that a part of herself was once lost, but now is found. Amazing Grace! She finally accepted that she had to take the developing action part of herself home within herself and integrate the little boy within her own mother and father introjects.

This woman was a consultant to customers of a large corporation. Much of the dream involved commercial theater and amusement parks because her work life was one area where she successfully used the little boy within herself to be more assertive. If she used too much of her emotional, i.e., feminine side, she found herself getting overly domineering and somewhat shrill with customers if things started to go awry, because she had too much **Shadow Queen** in her emotions. Her inner emotional power needed to be supplemented by the logical and assertive action part that was being developed within her psyche.

CHAPTER 17:
THE SAVAGE MASCULINE
ARCHETYPE

Key 17: The Savage Masculine is the action part of the psyche used for primitive defense.

We use the **Savage Masculine** for defensive purposes to do the dirty work in situations that demand a physically aggressive response. Such situations would involve combat, aggressive sports like boxing, or needing to defend oneself from a physically aggressive assailant. It is a Shadow part of the psyche which is easily recognized. Being subtle is not in the **Savage Masculine's** repertoire of possible responses. It is used in situations that demand physically aggressive responses now.

The **Savage Masculine** becomes a problem when it is used in inappropriate situations. It is a Shadow element that can easily get carried away. The appearance of the devil or some demonic entity is a sign that there is danger the **Savage Masculine** will get carried away. The danger occurs when the **Savage Masculine's** protective aggression goes over the top and becomes purely offensive, which is often the case with sociopaths.

DREAM 17A: GETTING AWAY FROM IT ALL

A 28-year-old man dreamt that he was on a ship that navigated to an island. When he went onto the island, there was a path covered with an elongated bamboo mat, which led to a vibrantly green and lush jungle. There was a large, muscular brute of a man blocking his way down the path.

The dream then shifted to him being on board an ocean liner, which was anchored near the island. There were two huge pipes going from the ocean liner to the island that were large enough for a man to walk in. The devil appeared and said that they each should race down a pipe to see who reached the island first. He then saw himself lying on the beach with the island in the distant horizon. A cloud formed over him and rained upon him.

DREAM 17A—INTERPRETATION

This was an early therapy dream. He was navigating his subconscious to find a new path in life. The bamboo paving the way to his growth is the recent growth within him that allowed him to even consider therapy. The lush jungle represented the new growth he was considering. The brute of a man was his previous macho man attitude, which was a strong **Savage Masculine** action part of the psyche. The devil in the dream emphasized the **Savage Masculine Shadow** because he had really "raised hell" when he was younger. His **Shadow** was encouraging him to race toward change and was trying to inspire his get up and go. The **Savage Masculine** is part of the "get up and go" that can inspire change now, not tomorrow.

Sitting on the beach meant that he was in the area between the subconscious ocean and conscious land, which is the semiconscious. He was backing away and distancing himself from therapy. The dream assured him that staying away from therapy would not be pleasant and would result in depression (represented by the rain.)

DREAM 17B: STAY AWAY FROM THAT MAN

The dreamer was a 52-year-old married woman. She was returning to her parents' house. Only her mother was in the house, with the doors locked. There was a scary man, who kept appearing episodically at the different windows. They then called the police, which was inconclusive. Nothing happened because the charges would not stick. The scary man was a large farmer with gangly arms and large ears. She then saw a waitress tackle the scary farmer. Later on she heard that some large football players beat the man up. The dreamer walked into the street of the town and saw Beefeaters (the guards at Buckingham Palace, known for their stoicism). The Beefeaters had their ornate red uniforms with large stovepipe furred hats. There was a guard on every street corner.

DREAM 17B—INTERPRETATION

The dream announced, at the beginning, that it was related to her earlier experiences when she lived at her parents' house. At the first level of dream interpretation, the various characters in the dream represent different parts of the dreamer's personality (the mind is projecting its various parts onto a condensed story). The mother introject in this dream (the mother image/model she carries now in her mind) typically represents part of the dreamer's emotional life. The dream was indicating that it was about her emotional responses.

The dreamer was haunted by a scary man who harassed her and the police were unable to do anything about it. When asked if she knew any football players, she noted, "I married one," as the husband she divorced in her youth, after only a year of marriage, played football in high school. They lived on a farm when they were married. Her former husband was suspected of shooting his second wife but nothing could be proven in court. The scary man and her former husband were the embodiment of the **Savage Masculine**.

The dream clearly warned her to stay away from her former husband. The gangly farm boy is tackled by a waitress because the dream is screaming, "Wait a minute!" She recently ran into her former husband at a high school reunion. He invited her to a street dance. She wisely declined.

The dream is strongly endorsing her decision with the Beefeater guards in the street. Their attitude and dress is direct advice to the dreamer to be sophisticated in her defenses (clothes represent defenses) and stoic in the face of the **Savage Masculine** former husband. The subconscious was being appropriately protective of her.

CHAPTER 18:
THE DIVINE CHILD ARCHETYPE

Key 18: The Divine Child Archetype is the portion of our psyche that holds our hopes and dreams for the future. She is often a little girl, roughly between the ages of five and eleven, with light-colored hair and blue eyes, as seen in Caucasian cultures. She is often a young girl with brown eyes and dark hair, as seen in Hispanic cultures. Other cultures will vary depending upon what are the considered ideal features of a young girl.

(Photo by Hung Chung Chih. September 28, 2012 in Kathmandu, Nepal. Kumari is a girl believed to be the incarnation of Hindu goddess Durga.)

The Divine Child frequently shows up in dreams, since people are most concerned about their futures. The Divine Child most often is a girl because it involves mainly our desired feelings for the future, i.e., it is the psyche's best guess of what needs to happen in the future to make us happy. Her appearance can mean that the dreamer is following the right course to some extent or needs to make adjustments and changes to realize the idealized emotions she wants in the future. The frequency and positivity of this archetype may partially explain why blondes are seen as attractive in Caucasian cultures. When the Divine Child appears in a dream, the question being raised by the dreamer is usually some variation of "What will make me happy in the future?"

Dream 18A: Venture Out Into the World

The dreamer was a 42-year-old divorcee who was starting a relationship. She dreamt that she went into a house. She prepared a cardboard box to store something. She put a towel in the bottom of the carton. Then she saw a little blue-eyed, blonde-haired girl who wanted to go into nature with her and have a picnic. Then, she suddenly decided to go talk to some teenagers.

Dream 18A—Interpretation

A house is often symbolic of the dreamer's own body or life. The dreamer was trying to "compartmentalize" by literally putting part of her life in a box. At the bottom of the box, she "threw in the towel" or tried to cushion the blow of what she was doing to the relationship by limiting it to sex and fondness. She was abused by men in the past and now insisted on being in control. She felt guilty about how her need for control affected the relationship. (In the dream, she wanted to soften the consequences of her actions with the towel.)

The blonde blue-eyed girl is the **Divine Child Archetype**. The motif of the **Divine Child** is that this is the child who will save us all and represents our hopes for the future. Her **Divine Child** wanted her to get in touch with her own nature and ground herself while also nurturing herself more (thus the picnic.) She was torn between compartmentalizing her life to be more in control in relationships and, on the other hand, considering taking a more expanded and nurturing view toward herself and her relationships.

Her going back to talk to teenagers meant that she wanted to address concerns dating back to her adolescence, when she was rebellious and a substance abuser. After she was raped, she decided to end the rebellious behavior by entering a twelve-step program in order to beat her addictions. The rape was a signature event in her life that led to her quashing her sexual desires. She wanted to direct the course of relationships so that she felt in some control of herself and life.

The **Divine Child** wanting her to venture out into the world was frightening to the point that she bolted back to wanting to address issues with men dating back at least to her adolescence.

Dream 18B: Following Divine Goals

A 27-year-old man dreamt that he was working at a Safeway grocery store. There was a managers' meeting that he was supposed to attend. Two women his age, Sarah and Ruth, were also supposed to attend the meeting. Sarah was a very aggressive woman, while Ruth was mellower. He later saw a little girl, about eight years old with blonde hair and blue eyes, walking in the area between the store and the checkout lines. He walked to where she was and she grabbed him and kissed him. She left the store, while he fled from her to the managers' meeting, where he was severely castigated for stealing from the store.

Dream 18B—Interpretation

He had recently been having difficulty with a long-term relationship. He worked at a retail store, where he was flirting with several attractive regular customers. The dream opened by indicating that it was going to present the "safe way" for him to deal with relationships. The dream is a "big" dream because it has the **Divine Child Archetype** in it. The **Divine Child** is often a girl roughly between the ages of five and eleven, who has blue eyes and blonde hair. The **Divine Child** represents all the hopes and aspirations the dreamer has for the future.

The aggressive and the passive women represented different parts of his emotions. He was conflicted as to whether to stay in a relationship that was not very fulfilling, or whether to more actively seek out a better long-term partner. The **Divine Child** kissing him (a sign of integration of the archetype with his psyche) before the checkout lines indicated that this part of his psyche wanted him to decide and integrate his relationship intentions before he died, i.e., before he "checked out."

Being castigated for stealing means being reprimanded for taking something that is not yours. His flirting was adding to the instability of his current relationship, so that what he was getting from working at the store was almost illegal in a feeling sense.

The **Divine Child** indicated that it wanted him to make some relationship decisions, to decide whether he was going to stay committed, before he "checks out" or dies. It was always his intention to be in a long-term relationship. He was, in a sense, stealing from his current relationship by flirting with attractive customers while not deciding whether to end his current relationship. He had part of his psyche castigating him for not making a decision before he "checks out" and for flirting with attractive customers. He thought the safe way was to stay in his current relationship while checking out attractive customers.

DREAM 18C: ANIMA WITH DIVINE TRAITS

A 36-year-old man dreamt that he, his brainy and somewhat nerdy younger brother, and the nicest male colleague at work set off from a beach to go across a lake. When they got to the other side, he decided to smoke some marijuana. The nicest guy in the office disappeared. He became upset when he went into a house that belonged to him, which had fireworks going off all around it in such a way that he thought he was under attack.

He got back into the boat and went up the shore to a hospital, which similarly had fireworks going off all around it. Located in a jungle, no damage was done to the hospital except for some minor brush fires to the surrounding foliage. He then had the vision of a beautiful blonde-haired blue-eyed woman nursing a small baby boy.

DREAM 18C—INTERPRETATION

Each person in the boat was a different part of his psyche. He was basically in the boat with his brains and his social self. Water is subconscious emotion and it being a lake indicated that it was localized emotion, which was more particular to him. Land is consciousness, while the beach is the semiconscious in between the subconscious water and conscious land. Through the characters that were included in the boat, the dream announced that it was about his brains and his social self at work. When he found his way through his emotions, which enabled him to navigate home, his first inclination was to smoke marijuana. This indicated that it was his inclination to avoid confrontation and isolate himself at work.

He felt he was personally (the fireworks occurred around his home) under attack when it was only a display of fireworks. There was much fire and noise at work from a visionary showman who was his immediate supervisor. This supervisor pushed the dreamer because he knew the dreamer was very talented. The dreamer's response was to recoil from the challenge, to take a laid back position and isolate himself (which is similar to the effect of marijuana.)

The last part of the dream was telling him that he needed to heal. We know this because he set off for a hospital, a place of healing. The dream once again told him what the problem was—he thought he was under attack, when all that was happening was a fiery and harmless display that was interfering with his growth. We know this because the hospital was in a jungle, a place of immense natural growth. That part of his growth is being affected is signified by brush being on fire.

The final image of a woman nursing a baby boy was telling him what needed to be done. His emotions needed to nurture a new part of himself that acted in a different way. The beautiful woman had elements of the **Divine Child Archetype** because of her physical features. Caucasian cultures typically see a blue-eyed blonde-haired child as representing their hopes and dreams for the future. The dream was asserting that he had the emotional resources to nurture new actions at work.

CHAPTER 19:
THE WILLING SACRIFICE

Key 19: The Willing Sacrifice is a person who is ready to sacrifice or give his life in service for the good of others. In its positive manifestation, it is true altruism. In its negative form, it is a maladaptive pattern of behavior often drilled into the person by their upbringing.

DREAM 19A: LIGHT MY FIRE

A 38-year-old man dreamt that he was at an ashram, or temple, in India run by his mother. He was lying in the "healing waters" when the woman, his mother, suddenly set fire to the nearby sacred food. An overriding voice warned him not to accept responsibility for the fire, which he was prone to do.

DREAM 19A—INTERPRETATION

The sacred and archetypal nature of the dream was announced by the setting, which was an ancient culture where millenniums of sacred practices were performed. Great cultures are firmly entrenched in the "collective unconscious," since we or our predecessors were exposed to these cultures. When there are elements of an ancient culture in a dream, these patterns of thought, or archetypes, are firmly fastened to the collective unconscious that we all share.

Water in a dream is virtually always emotions or subconscious forces. The dreamer was trying to heal himself when his mother set the sacred food on fire. This is the negative mother introject being malevolent in destroying food because it usually represents psychological support or nourishment. The negative mother introject within him spoiled his food or nourishment so that he ended up getting burned. Fire gives the additional meaning that he needs to change (fire changes matter into kinetic energy).

The overriding voice warned him not to be a **Willing Sacrifice**. He had years of suffering because he was chronically ready to take responsibility for events that were not his fault. When he was growing up, in a desperate attempt to convince her to nurture him, he accepted the role of "fall guy" or scapegoat for his mother. He needed to free himself from the despotic distortion of his reality.

DREAM 19B: SPIT FIRE

A 48-year-old teacher dreamt that she was on a spit being cooked outdoors over a fire. A crowd of people were around her, taking pieces of her off the spit as it rotated.

DREAM 19B—INTERPRETATION

She was being forced to eliminate creativity from her teaching. She was told to teach according to what was likely to be on a yearly achievement test. She felt that she was being forced to change and had no say in the matter, which was like being held over a fire while pieces of her went to nurture others at her expense. This is like the **Willing Sacrifice Archetype**, only she was a **not-so-Willing Sacrifice**. She literally felt that the job was tearing her apart. Fire was involved because it signals change. In this case, it signified forced change that really burned her up to the point that she was fit to spit.

Chapter 20:
The Wise Old Man
Archetype

Key 20: The Wise Old Man is a therapeutic part of the father introject that gives common sense advice about what you may want to do.

Dream 20A: The Party Is Not Over

A 61-year-old woman dreamt that she went to an old employer's home. When she went in, she saw what she thought was the aftermath of a party. The celebrants insisted that the party was not over. They wanted her to stay and join the party. She thought she should go back to her job as a nurse. She also thought she should go to physical therapy instead of being at the party. Her kind boss tried to convince her that her work did not need her and that she should tone down her physical therapy efforts.

Dream 20A—Interpretation

Her old employer was a kind and generous man who did not micromanage her work and relied on her to make many daily decisions. He was very supportive, and she viewed him as one of the best bosses that she had ever had. She was now working as a nurse

and was being given increasing supervisory roles without getting any increase in pay. This was in spite of her having increasing physical problems. She went to physical therapy, but she frustrated her physical therapist because she insisted on repetitive exercise to the point that the physical therapist asked her to be less hardcore. She literally was tearing her body down with too much exercise.

Her old employer was the embodiment of the **Wise Old Man**. The dream was using the **Wise Old Man** because she was more likely to believe this part of her psyche. Her subconscious was using the **Wise Old Man** to deliver the message that she should focus less on work and take it easier in her healing efforts, which at this point were counterproductive. She needed to be more social and have fun, because she was wrong in assuming that the party was over. Being male, the **Wise Old Man** virtually always offers advice on what actions the dreamer could take or avoid that would serve the dreamer's best interests.

DREAM 20B: LEAVE IT BEHIND ALREADY

A 34-year-old man dreamt that he was talking with his wife on a balcony in a hotel. She had no clothes on and suddenly jumped backwards off the balcony. He ran down to see what condition she was in. They were on the second floor and there was grass below the balcony. He found her unhurt and naked. He returned to the balcony and looked over a courtyard outside of the hotel. He then entered the elevator and found himself going to a lower floor with three females that were employed at the previous firm where he was employed. He reached the lower floor, where he found an older man who advised him that he should return to his own floor because the older man was going to seal the lower floors shut so that the dreamer would not need to ever enter these lower floors again.

DREAM 20B—INTERPRETATION

The dream occurred in a hotel, which is a commercial establishment, indicating that the dream was referring to a business situation. His significant other, his wife, represented his emotions. His emotions surprised him. The fact that his wife was not hurt indicated that his fears of something unexpected and negative happening were making him feel emotionally vulnerable (his wife being without clothing indicated that the dreamer felt emotionally exposed and vulnerable), to the point that his fears were unwarranted. His looking over a courtyard was due to legal action being taken by his old company, i.e., court. That he went up an elevator with females from the old company indicated that he was trying to take his emotions regarding the old company to a higher level. That there were three females was significant because three is the number of change. The dream was telling him that he needed to change by taking his emotions to a higher level. The older man was the **Wise Old Man Archetype**. His inner **Wise Old Man** was reassuring him that this portion of his psyche would take care of the past emotions from his old company. The dreamer was being told that he need not concern himself with such emotions and that he should return to his own life and marriage. The past was literally going to be destroyed according to the dream, and the dreamer did not need to concern himself with it.

CHAPTER 21:
MODE OF TRANSPORTATION

Key 21: The mode of transportation in a dream makes a statement about how the dreamer is moving through his or her life.

Vehicles are how we get somewhere in life, and that is much of their meaning in dreams. A car is the most frequent metaphorical symbol of modern life. It is freedom in many ways, because you can go almost anywhere you want in the immediate vicinity.

It is important whether the dreamer is a driver or a passenger. The driver has more control. Like life, minor adjustments in how you steer your car or course in life make major differences in terms of where you will end up.

The passenger is relatively passive, being "taken for a ride." If the dreamer is in the backseat, this emphasizes a lack of control. It may even be a criticism or a summary of the situation of the dreamer's life. He might criticize the drivers of his life course too much. In that case, he is in danger of becoming a "backseat driver."

Dreams frequently point to the driver's general approach to life. Does the dreamer like to take the highway (high way) of doing things, or is the dreamer more interested in freedom (the free way)? Dreams point out whether the dreamer is reckless by the speed, swerves, crashes, and disregarded stoplights and stop signs. Prominent yellow stoplights can be a cry for using greater caution.

Buses are a means of communal travel and signify how well the person is going along with the crowd, which can be, of course, beneficial or harmful. Trains are a frequent symbol in dreams, although modern travelers in the United States do not utilize the train very much at this time. Trains are such an excellent symbol of one's course in life, though, that even modern dreams use this symbol with amazing frequency.

Trains match many circumstances in modern life, i.e., we frequently wonder if we are "on the right track." The train leaves at a specific time, as if it were fated. The train waits or stops for no man. If someone wanders onto the track of a train, it does not stop because it must go on. It cannot consider the circumstances of every wanderer, as the primary goal of progress with the train is the higher or communal good. It is the individual's responsibility to not get run over by life. One frequently wonders whether a decision was made in time or did "that train already leave the station?" We all look for "light at the end of the tunnel" and hope that it is not an oncoming train.

I had a clinical psychology professor, Dr. Jack Watkins, who was a master hypnotist. His books exemplify the **Wise Old Man Archetype** (Watkins, 1982). He died in 2012 at the age of 98 years old. The last one of his eleven books was published around 2008. He would sometimes regress a client to an earlier time in life by using hypnosis. After the hypnotic induction, he would have the person visualize that they were seated in a train that was traveling backwards. Each mile that they traveled backwards took them further back into past memories.

The defined course of a train seems like life. Like life, there are critical decision points where you can decide to switch tracks or remain on the same course. This is a combination of the fated and free will view of life. Certain decisions point you in a direction that is difficult to change. You often have to wait for the right time to make a critical decision regarding whether you should "switch tracks" or not.

Bridges are interesting because they virtually always point to a major passage in the person's life. The bridge is on land and most frequently extends over water, which is most often a river (which usually is the river of life.) The bridge or passage is being traversed consciously in order to navigate one's way over harrowing emotional waters. It signals a major transition in life.

DREAM 21A: GET OUT OF TOWN

A 38-year-old man dreamt he was driving a Ferrari car and that he passed his brother and sister, who were also driving a Ferrari. They waved pleasantly to him. He then saw himself driving the Ferrari up a rickety wooden staircase that reached high into the sky. He parked the car at the height of the heavens and then went halfway down the stairway and turned to his left, where he saw his parents' home. They did not want him to come into the house, but wished him well in his travels. He went to his Ferrari and drove it down the staircase. He was then in his hometown, and he was racing to the main exit out of town, where he had to take a right turn. Another race car, which was approaching the intersection from the opposite direction, took the turn from the left and fell in behind him as they hastily tore out of town.

DREAM 21A—INTERPRETATION

He was the lead singer in a rock band. He thought maybe he should think of having a relationship with children involved, but it never worked out. He just really was not into children, which partially was due to his having a harsh and critical father. Things were changing rapidly in his life (he was becoming a rock star), which is why the fast cars were involved. His brother and sister were indicative of the shared values they were taught as kids, which included the traditional family. They wished him well as he searched for his dreams. He, in fact, climbed the "stairway to heaven," which is a rock song by Led Zeppelin. He parked his car at the top of the stairway and literally had a "comedown" when he considered joining his family's way of life. These family parts of himself knew that they were not his ultimate dream. He "came down to earth" and raced away from his hometown values, with his conscious (coming from the right) leading his subconscious (coming from the left.) The conscious is associated with the right and the subconscious is associated with the left. The dream was screaming that his favored values were elsewhere, rather than the hometown values he was handed.

DREAM 21B: BEATING THE TRAIN OF LIFE

A 28-year-old man dreamt that he was driving a car downhill on a San Francisco street. Near the bottom of the hill was a railroad crossing. There was a train approaching from the right. He knew that he could get down the hill in time to beat the train. To his left was a gunman shooting at a policeman near a store on his right. He knew that he could make it in time.

DREAM 21B—INTERPRETATION

Movement downhill usually represents movement toward the subconscious. He always wanted to live in San Francisco or a heavily populated city. Trains frequently represent the progression of life as it is on a fixed or fatalistic course to some extent, although the train can slow down, speed up, go backwards or change tracks. This was at a critical point in his life, where he knew he had to make a decision before it was too late. He was confident because he knew he could beat a deadline. The gunman shooting at the policeman represented his subconscious shooting down of his superego or conscience, which is represented by the policeman. His shooting at the policeman indicated that he had excess superego and guilt regarding commercial interests that he needed to eliminate. He was always very conflicted about making money. This was a critical point in his life where he needed to take dramatic steps before options were closed to him, represented by the train blocking his way eventually.

DREAM 21C: THE DISTANCER

A 37-year-old man dreamt that he and his high school friends were having a heated discussion. Bruce was the friend who was tall, dark and handsome, while his friend Lenny was book smart, responsible, and isolated, always preferring to withdraw from social contact. They were arguing about how to approach social situations. Bruce was much more socially skilled and usually had attractive women near him seventy percent of the time. Lenny never dated. The dreamer left the discussion, while the argument between his socially skilled friend and his book smart friend continued.

The dream then shifted to him sitting on a chair mounted on top of a train, above the engine. To his left was a group of neatly dressed black people. They threw rocks at the train so that the dreamer feared for his safety, held up his arms, and avoided looking at them. The people were always on the left side of the train. As the train rounded a bend, the group of black people became angrier and appeared disheveled. One elderly black woman somehow made it to where he was seated and reached for his genitals. He responded by putting a plastic bowl over his genitals.

DREAM 21C—INTERPRETATION

As males, his two friends represented action parts of himself. He had a Bruce side to his personality that could be very social, but which he generally avoided using. The Lenny part of his personality was the smart nose-to-the-grindstone loner, which he used at work. The discussion between the two friends is due to his desire to use the often neglected social part of his personality.

The second part of the dream told us why he avoided using this social part of himself. Trains are a frequent metaphor as to whether the dreamer is on the right track in life. That he is in a chair on top of the train, exposed to the elements and possible rock throwing, represents his feeling vulnerable to people who want to be closer to him. They are on the left side of the train because the left side tends to represent subconscious material. The darker the skin, the more soul and intimacy is being called for. The crowd degenerates into a shadowy and more threatening crowd as he persists in avoiding looking at and acknowledging the soulful parts of himself, which is what the black people represented. He did not allow others to get close to him because he feared getting hurt.

There were parts of his emotional **Shadow**, represented by the elderly black woman, that were frustrated with his reluctance to the point of threatening castration (castration anxiety). His response was to be phony and superficial, which was symbolized by him covering his genitals with a plastic bowl. The dream was being dramatic and used subconscious fear to exaggerate a warning to get him to change his social interaction withdrawal.

CHAPTER 22:
INTEGRATION

Key 22: Trees, marriage and having sex are signs that the individual is integrating. The gathering of a diverse group of people at a table, especially if the table is round (since a circle involves the soul, because it has no beginning and no end) indicates that for the various and different parts of the psyche, integration is "on the table."

Trees are a major symbol of integration in dreams. It is a living thing that grows. It is with you on the ground, its roots extend deep into the ground, and it opens up to the sky. This symbol of growth unites the three major realms, which correspond with the subconscious, the ego, and the superego.

Dr. Carl Jung was a psychiatrist who was an early follower of Freud in the early part of the twentieth century. He and Freud eventually disagreed on many matters. Jung eventually started his own school of psychoanalytic thought which relied heavily on dream interpretation. For Jung, mental health was about integration of the masculine and feminine portions of the psyche for both females and males. Marriage for Jung symbolized integration of the masculine portions of the psyche with the feminine portions.

Having access to both genders increases adaptability, as the person then has a wide range of emotions and actions from which to choose. Sexual intercourse means that the dreamer's actions are integrating with the dreamer's emotions. Sex means that the masculine is integrating with the feminine, that actions are congruent with emotions. This union of masculine and feminine portions of the psyche is cooperative and positive with a pervasive sharing of goals. Orgies are integration on a geometric scale, with many of the dreamer's actions now integrating with various emotions.

DREAM 22A: PLAY BALL

A 47-year-old man dreamt that he saw an old man pick up a branch from a tree on the ground. The old man threw the branch out into a bay. When the branch reached the deep bottom of the water, multitudes of footballs floated to the surface. He saw the footballs float off into the distant sky. He felt sure that there were still plenty of footballs left at the bottom of the bay.

DREAM 22A—INTERPRETATION

He was very competitive and aggressive in sports when he was young. He was in therapy and was trying to become more social and less aggressive. The old man was similar in age to the therapist. This was the **Wise Old Man Archetype**, which is psychologically insightful and offers advice. The broken branch was an old part of a tree, which indicated that his subconscious was talking about a part of his psychological functioning in the past. Water is subconscious emotion, with the depths of the water representing the depths of the psyche. The footballs represented his deeply competitive and aggressive spirit. The dream urged him to let go of some of that attitude, which was symbolized by the footballs floating away. The dream assured him at the end that there were still plenty of footballs and competitive spirit left in his psychological makeup.

DREAM 22B: YOU MUST BE OUT OF YOUR TREE

A 52-year-old woman dreamt that she was digging a fir tree out of the snow. The tree was about eight feet tall and the bottom four feet of the tree were icy. The tree became her Christmas tree. She then saw herself disposing of the tree after the holidays. The tree was very dry and desiccated. It still had decorative Christmas balls hanging from it, with pictures of animals on each one. She carefully preserved these Christmas balls. She then saw herself in a mobile home, which was surrounded and supported by a gigantic tree. Inside the house, every item she owned, such as chairs, tables, and dishware, came in sets of four.

DREAM 22B—INTERPRETATION

A tree is a major symbol of integration and growth because its roots extend far into the earth, it is present on the ground, and it opens up to the sky. Water is emotion, and snow is frozen water, which metaphorically is frozen or cold emotion. The Christmas tree uncovering was saying that she needed to bring her life out of a deep freeze and celebrate (which is the reason for the inclusion of the holidays). Animals represent instincts, and the dream was saying that she needed to save, honor and preserve her more showy or flamboyant instincts. The particular decoration may refer to male anatomy or encouragement to be involved sexually. In any case, she had a crisis situation with a supervisor at work where she had to "show some balls" to avoid being fired.

The final scenes referred to her being in the process of moving to a new residence, which is why the house is "mobile." The dream signaled that this move would be central to her integration, which is why a tree surrounds the mobile home. Four is the number of stability, as tables and chairs have four legs, there are four seasons, there are four directions, and there are four quarters to every game. The dream strongly indicated the need for her to make stable decisions to continue her integration.

DREAM 22C: GROWING UP

A 19-year-old woman dreamt that her grandmother, mother and favorite aunt were sitting around a backyard fireplace located next to a huge tree. Suddenly a two-year old boy appeared and her favorite aunt encouraged her to take care of him.

DREAM 22C—INTERPRETATION

The dream announced that it was about her integration as a woman. The presence of a tree with three important adult female relatives specifically pointed to the dream being about her integration as a woman. The fireplace was important because fire is metaphorically a symbol of change and transformation (it changes matter into energy). The little boy was a part of the dreamer that represented her actions. It was a young child because her ability to act independently was relatively new. The dream was about her integration and transformation into doing things that some young adult women do.

DREAM 22D: PATIENCE BABY

A 33-year-old woman dreamt that she married someone other than her husband. The man was a friend who was known for his great patience. Her husband simultaneously had a dream that same night that his wife became pregnant with a baby girl.

DREAM 22D—INTERPRETATION

Marriage is a major symbol of the integration of male with female, of actions with emotions. The woman's dream indicated integration of her emotions with a new way of doing things. She simply wanted to do things in a more patient way. Marriage, and, in fact, any type of consensual positive sex, was seen by followers of Jung as integration of the dreamer's actions (primarily masculine energy) with the dreamer's emotions (primarily feminine energy). As we saw in Dream 1A at the beginning of this book, an orgy can indicate that many different actions (men) are integrating with many different emotions (women).

Her husband, dreaming that his wife was pregnant with a girl, indicated that he anticipated the arrival of a new emotional part of himself. It was also a condensation of the fact that he wanted his wife to have a baby. It represented him anticipating emotional growth on his part if his wife had the desired and hoped-for infant. Her husband was very impatient with the whole process. The woman's dream was a condensation of the fact that she wished she were more patient and especially, that her husband showed more patience. This therapist found it to be a frequent occurrence that couples can have related dreams because they are often dealing with related issues.

CHAPTER 23:
COLOR MY WORLD

Key 23: Color indicates emotional issues are involved in the dream.

Color gives us the emotional tone of a dream. In projective personality tests such as the Rorschach Inkblot test, where the psychologist asks the examinee to make shapes out of ambiguous forms, if the examinee notices  or uses color a lot, it is assumed that the emotional content of the person's psychological state is being revealed subconsciously. In actuality, dreams are literally projections manufactured by the subconscious.

◘ Red can be either love or anger, depending upon the context. Eastern philosophy places red with the first chakra (you are sitting on your first chakra). Eastern views are that the first chakra goes with family, or more accurately, tribal loyalty. It is the most basic chakra and it goes with red-blooded loyalty, which is why the strongest emotions (love and anger) are seen as belonging to this chakra. Red signals that serious tribal emotions are involved. Red stoplights can be a directive to cease and desist.

◻ Orange goes with the second chakra, which is the sexual chakra. When orange appears prominently in a dream, sexual issues are usually lurking somewhere in the mix.

◻ Yellow is the color of self-esteem and goes with the third chakra, which is in the solar plexus. In keeping with traffic lights, yellow can be a color of caution.

◻ Gold indicates that something precious or valuable to the dreamer is involved. It frequently means that there are elements from the dreamer's past that could be valuable. The gold may be found at the bottom of the ocean, in a cave, or in a basement. These locations confirm that the dreamer is searching his or her subconscious for valuables. Similarly, searching through a warehouse or closet often signals that the dreamer is taking stock of what parts or lessons from the past should be kept or discarded. Discovery of gold or jewels in such a setting can be a sign that the dreamer found gold within herself.

◻ Pink is the color of affection. It is not great love but is similar to the positive feeling one has toward a family pet.

◻ Green is the color of growth, the color of plants. In Eastern philosophy, green goes with the fourth chakra, located in the heart. The heart chakra was seen as integrating the three lower chakras with the three higher and more mental/metaphysical chakras. Green lights can sometimes be the "go" light for a given project.

◻ Blue is my favorite color and has a multiplicity of meanings, depending upon context. It is the color of the sky. When paired with green, it can be seen as giving flight and freedom to emerging growth. Blue was seen in Eastern philosophy as going with the throat chakra and as being related to speech and creativity. It was considered to involve mental processes. On the other hand, blue could represent depression, i.e., a person feeling "blue."

◻ Purple was considered to go with the highest chakra. It frequently denotes royalty or an honorable passage in life, such as graduation.

◻ White is the most spiritual of all the colors and represents our highest aspirations. Goodness and all that is pure frequently goes with white. Spiritual issues, wholeness and expanded consciousness are frequently involved.

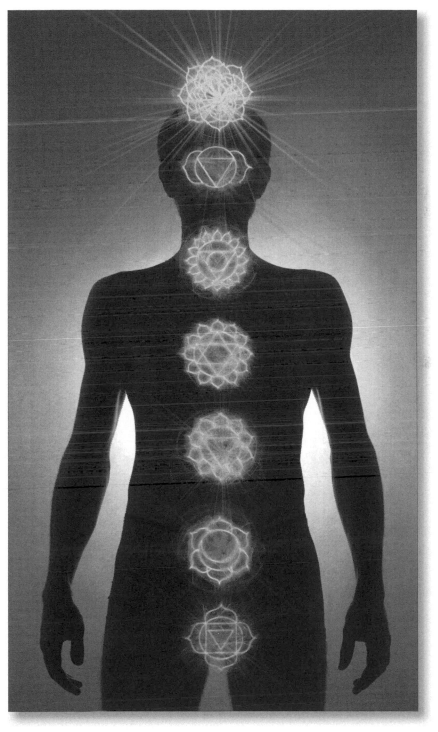

◻ Black almost always indicates **Shadow** issues, i.e., death, depression or decay. A completely dark figure in profile usually indicates **Shadow**. These meanings are not to be confused with racial color. Dreams clearly indicate that the darker the skin, the more soul is being called for, i.e., we even call it "soul" music.

DREAM 23A: CONQUERING ABUSE AFTEREFFECTS

A 17-year-old girl dreamt that she was being chased by a prehistoric black monster that was very ugly and threatening, with sharp teeth. The monster chased her to the edge of a cliff. She jumped off the cliff to escape the monster and felt like she almost died. As she fell, she kept falling down a deep abyss surrounded by colorful lights. She hit the bottom face-first into a pool of water.

She was able to turn around and float on her back. The dream then continued with her dreaming that she was getting married and was being carried to the altar by her fiancé.

DREAM 23A—INTERPRETATION

She was severely physically and sexually abused as a child for many years. The prehistoric black monster indicated her blinding **Shadow** rage from the abuse that consistently interfered with relationships. That the monster is prehistoric is perfect in the sense that the rage went as far back in her personal history as she could remember. That the monster was black signaled that her **Shadow** was the main part of her psyche that was outraged. Her jumping off the cliff indicated that she wanted the rage to end. It was also a condensation of her desire to "fly away" from the rage and aftereffects of the abuse.

That she was falling into a deep abyss indicated that she was trying to deal with the issues buried deep in her subconscious. The colorful lights simply indicated that all shades of her emotions were actively and vividly involved in the changes she was making. She "hit bottom" when she fully faced her emotional struggles (she hit the water, emotion, face first). She was able to cope with this emotional trauma because she was integrating masculine and feminine, action and emotion, parts of her psyche (marriage is a primary indicator of integrating masculine and feminine, action and emotion, within the psyche). Her being carried by her fiancé is a condensation of her feeling supported by her own actions and her feeling loved and supported by her fiancé.

DREAM 23B: DOING TOO MUCH FOR OTHERS

A 52-year-old woman dreamt she was being asked by her father to give him three minutes to let him tell her something. He then told her that her favorite aunt had a blood test, which indicated that she had cancer. An overriding voice in the dream proclaimed, "She did too much for others and not enough for herself." The aunt was a lively and vivacious person who consistently put her needs last to try to help others be happy.

DREAM 23B—INTERPRETATION

The number three is a number of change because three people in a relationship is an unstable dynamic where almost always one of the three feels on the outside. Things are surely going to change. So the dream was announcing that this dream was going to be about changing her actions because the message was delivered by her father introject, which typically represents the action part of a person (not necessarily so, but that is usually the way it falls out after thousands of years of culture). Red and blood are associated with the first chakra, which is the seat of family or tribal allegiance. Loyalty to the family means looking out for yourself, as that is usually also in the best interests of the family. Her father introject is telling her by metaphor that one should not neglect their own needs too much for the sake of others. Cancer is often contracted by people who are too nice, to the extent that their immune system does not recognize the parasitic invader and thus does not dispose of it, resulting in the person's own harm. The overriding voice indicated that it was a message straight from her unconscious, higher self or soul— whichever, as they are more or less referring to the same thing.

DREAM 23C: LOVE ME TENDER

A 20-year-old man dreamt that he was surfing in the ocean. The waves were higher than normal, but he felt he could handle them. Next to him on another surfboard was a muscular man with a large tattoo of a cat on his back. When they made it to shore, the scene shifted to a restaurant, where the dreamer became the muscular surf boarder. He gave his girlfriend, Elizabeth, a white cat.

DREAM 23C—INTERPRETATION

The ocean is the most significant symbol of subconscious emotion we have. That there were huge waves in the dream indicated there was a lot of emotional turbulence with which he had to deal. His surfing competently meant that he was riding out the emotional turbulence successfully. The best news was the appearance of the **Heroic Masculine** in the form of a dashing muscular man, which represented a significant portion of his psyche. Cats represent female affection. That the **Heroic Masculine** part of his psyche had a large tattoo on his back meant that this portion of his psyche allowed a female's affection to get under his skin. Elizabeth was the woman with whom he was entranced, and he wanted to receive nourishment from her, as indicated by his going to a restaurant to meet with her. White is a spiritual and sacred color. His giving her the cat represented his wanting to have a nourishing and spiritually fulfilling relationship with her. The dreamer would benefit substantially from this integration of the masculine and feminine if the relationship worked out as he hoped.

DREAM 23D: BURSTING MY BUBBLE

A 56-year-old man dreamt that he met an extremely beautiful woman. He was in his thirties in the dream. He felt deeply emotional and felt total gratitude toward the woman. He then saw himself viewing the world from behind a partially constructed prison wall.

The dream then shifted to his seeing himself let go of thousands of balloons of every imaginable vivid color within a city. The balloons were driven by the wind into various structures in the city. Whatever structures the balloons ran into were destroyed. Finally, when the last balloon burst, the city was destroyed and disappeared from view.

DREAM 23D—INTERPRETATION

When he was in his thirties, he finally realized that he was an alcoholic. He joined AA and felt that he changed emotionally. The beautiful woman in the dream represented his newly-gained emotional outlook at that time. He was very grateful for the emotional changes, which were reflected in the first part of the dream. He tended to get stuck emotionally and hang onto cherished emotional insights even after they had run their course and were no longer useful. He found he frequently avoided even positive emotional changes. He would stay in the comfort of the often-stagnant walls he built around himself, which imprisoned him in a fortress of solitude.

Bright colors frequently represent emotions in a dream. The emotions are his since he was holding onto the balloons before they went airborne. He thought that the original emotional epiphany he gained from AA would last forever; however, that was not the case. He found that every so many years, he would have additional insights that greatly influenced his feelings.

The city being destroyed by the balloons was reflective of the fact that when he let his emotions soar too much (he was prone to manic episodes), his world literally came crashing down around him. Also, his hard-won epiphanies often almost completely changed his emotional reactions. The city being devoured by the balloons was partially reflective of his manic episodes corroding his world. Additionally, new AA insights gathered through the years that had significant emotional impact upon him meant that he had to build a new world. Every so many years, his bubbles (balloons/emotions) were burst, and that deconstructed his then-current world view. He found that life was indeed a journey of emotional changes and not a fixed and static city in his mind.

CHAPTER 24:
CONSCIOUS AND
SUBCONSCIOUS ELEMENTS

Key 24: Dreams give clues and guidelines as to whether an unconscious conflict or conscious behavior is being addressed by the dream. Different elements of the dream indicate whether one is addressing conscious or subconscious issues.

If the dream indicates that it is occurring during daylight, conscious issues are being addressed. If the dream specifies a nighttime event, subconscious issues are being addressed. In line with Eastern philosophies, the right side of the body goes with the conscious and the left side of the body goes with the subconscious.

Movement downward many times means that the dreamer is going deeper into subconscious issues. Going to the bottom of the ocean, going underground or to a basement, or going into a cave similarly frequently represent movement toward the subconscious.

The ocean is the overwhelming primordial symbol of the subconscious. Lakes, rivers, and swimming pools each indicate slightly different types of emotions or subconscious energy. Lakes indicate more personal and localized events in the dreamer's life. Rivers tend to represent the flow of life. Swimming pools are largely subconscious emotions in reaction to other people in our personal domestic lives.

Land tends to be more conscious issues, in contrast to the emotional or subconscious issues associated with bodies of water. Beaches are the area where subconscious and conscious issues interface and are the semiconscious, if you will. A person strolling down a beach in a dream typically is trying to resolve how to integrate conscious and subconscious issues for the good of the dreamer.

If the dream contains parts where the dreamer sees either herself or sees important characters asleep, this is usually a sign that subconscious contents are being examined or evaluated by the dreamer. In the movie "The Wizard of Oz," Dorothy and her three companions fall asleep in a poppy field before entering Oz. This dreamlike movie was announcing that the fantastic city of Oz was created by the subconscious. As in life, like the movie, the main character would make her way through the subconscious maze with her brains, heart and courage to find her home in the world.

DREAM 24A: STUFFING FEELINGS

A 32-year-old woman dreamt that she was on a hill. She walked down the hill to a highway. She was selling her lunch and other personal food items to passersby. A man driving a large truck went by her a short distance and then stopped on the side of the road. A large man got out of the truck and was running back to her. He put out his hand and congratulated her with, "Hallelujah, you finally did it!"

DREAM 24A—INTERPRETATION

Movement downward usually means that the dreamer is going down within herself to deal with subconscious emotion. The dreamer had an eating disorder and was a binge eater. She avoided eating before therapy sessions because if she were satiated with food she put up the front that "everything is all right" and avoided talking about her real feelings. Money is energy in dreams. The dream was assuring her that if she gets rid of some of her food, she will gain energy. The truck driver is the action part of her, assuring her that by getting rid of her extreme focus on food, she will be able to make more significant moves in her life. His appearance in the dream is good news. (A truck carries heavy loads, which the action executive driver can deliver almost anywhere.) The dream was assuring her that the positive and strong action part of her psyche could deliver the goods to most any portion of her life.

DREAM 24B: THAT'S SOME WINNEBAGO YOU HAVE

A 47-year-old alcoholic man in recovery dreamt that he and another recovering alcoholic that he knew through AA were driving a Winnebago. The other man was a similar age and worked as an engineer. They were fixing up the Winnebago as it was moving so that it could fly, go on land, and also travel on water. They went to the top of a cliff and the Winnebago became airborne and glided down to the lake below. The Winnebago was immersed in water. When it came up out of the water, it continued boating toward a not-too-distant shore.

DREAM 24B—INTERPRETATION

A Winnebago is a traveling house. It is literally a house on the move. A house can represent the dreamer himself. He was literally trying to engineer himself so that he could be spiritual (fly), deal with subconscious emotion (water), and consciously put his changes into action (land). He was not quite ready to fly, but could engineer a softer landing for the impact of his emotions on his home, which was in transition (the Winnebago). He was immersed in water and successfully came up from this immersion in subconscious emotion, with the implication that he was moving toward conscious awareness (land) that informed his behavior and choices. Interpersonally, the dream signaled major changes for him at home, as the home situation was in transition (the Winnebago was always in motion).

DREAM 24C: GO EAST, YOUNG MAN

A 22-year-old man incubated a dream (incubation is described in chapter 34) in which he asked whether he should transfer to a school in California. He dreamt that he was in the ocean in California surfing. He was trying to catch a wave, but every time he stood up, he fell flat on his face. He then saw himself in Alaska, phoning a woman that he knew in California. He noted that he was doing well in Alaska, had quit drinking, and then wished the woman well.

DREAM 24C—INTERPRETATION

Being in the ocean surfing near the California coast meant that he was consulting his subconscious, as the ocean is the largest known symbol of the subconscious. He was trying to navigate his way to California, but literally could not stand on his own two feet. His subconscious was commenting that he was not ready for California.

His phoning the woman was his subconscious making peace with the part of his emotions that really wanted to go to California. He wished these emotions well and explained that he couldn't go to California in order to avoid worsening his excessive drinking. The dream recommended that he "chill" (go to Alaska) because being less anxious reduced his drinking. He decided not to go to California and was able to curtail his drinking, which had become a problem. He realized he needed to wait for a later time, when he would be more prepared to catch the proper emotional wave to California.

DREAM 24D: MY LIFE GOES OUT TO SEA

A 38-year-old woman dreamt that she was on a beach. Her feet were riveted to and stuck in one place in the sand. In the ocean, she could see her high school boyfriend being swept out to sea. She felt powerless to help him, but felt that he would make it to shore somehow.

DREAM 24D—INTERPRETATION

She was stuck between her subconscious (the ocean) and her conscious (the land) in her semiconscious (the beach) and felt helpless. Her high school boyfriend was the embodiment of the **Heroic Masculine**, as he was always kind, considerate and protective of her. In the dream, he represented the positive action part of herself, which she felt was being overwhelmed by her subconscious emotions. She was raped repeatedly by a stepfather as a child and she found herself having aversion to her husband whom she married for convenience, as he was a wealthy businessman. He somehow reminded her of the stepfather, for which there was no rational or logical basis.

Despite these feelings being illogical, she felt unable to control them, which is why she started therapy. She felt unable to connect with the positive action part of herself (represented by her good high school boyfriend) in this situation. Her feeling out of control is epitomized in the dream by the positive action part of herself being swept away by her subconscious. She was immobilized in the dream, which reflected her feeling of being unable to reconcile her marriage to a man she really loved. She still had hope, which was manifested in the dream as the belief that the **Heroic Masculine** boyfriend would somehow make it to shore.

Chapter 25:
Nourishment and Nurture

Key 25: The primary symbol dreams use to signal nourishment, both physically and psychologically, is food.

When food comes into the picture in a dream, the subconscious in one form or another is discussing how the dreamer is being nurtured or not. The kitchen signals domestic or homegrown nurturing and frequently involves family and/or significant others, but may also involve friends. The kitchen is also a place of creativity, since various meals and food are creatively prepared there. It is interesting that the subconscious ties creativity with nourishment. This writer, as a result of personal experience, believes that to be creative, one has to be nurtured and also, preferably, finds creative activities nurturing.

When one encounters royal or medieval banquets in a dream, the subconscious is deriving its symbols from the collective unconscious. These dreams, in particular, are likening classic nurturing to the dreamer's situation. Archetypal elements such as these are frequently a sign that the dream is "big" and has important information to dispense to the dreamer.

Frequently, issues of nurture in dreams are being worked out at a restaurant. Persons in attendance are different parts of the person's psyche gathering together to resolve issues in the best interests of the dreamer. Grocery stores hold food and are typically warehouses of nurture in dreams. The issues usually involve how the dreamer is going to find and secure satisfying nurture. Adulterated food is frequently used in dreams to point out behavior that is not good for the dreamer, i.e., such as food spoiled with drugs, pointing to the need for the dreamer to quit abusing drugs.

DREAM 25A: RESERVATIONS, PLEASE

A 42-year-old man dreamt that he made reservations at a restaurant for himself and his wife. When they arrived at the restaurant, he noticed that they were second on the list; however, couple after couple were going ahead of them. When he talked to the hostess, she assured him that the section they were going to be seated in was closed for now, so that the other couples were being seated in other sections not available to him. He tried to convince the hostess that this was ridiculous, but the hostess kept insisting that it was merely restaurant policy. He noticed a bar to his right.

DREAM 25A—INTERPRETATION

The dream announced that it was going to be about how he and his wife nurtured each other. The dream made the initial comment that he had reservations about how they related to one other. One problem was that he was feeling like he was continually being placed second on his wife's list of priorities. He also felt like they could not get on the same page as to where they were going, either for entertainment or, more importantly, where they were going in life. He felt excluded and delayed, without being heard.

The bar at the end of the dream indicated that drinking was an issue. He recently stopped drinking because of his wife's complaints. Every detail in a dream means something. The dream interpreter does well to take each symbol seriously. The subconscious packs the maximum amount of meaning possible into a dream. The often strange symbols in dreams are designed to condense as much meaning as possible into a dream. The often peculiar images produced by the subconscious may be a desperate effort to get the dreamer's attention.

DREAM 25B: GOOD ON YOU

A 52-year-old woman dreamt that she was leading a crowd of people to a fancy restaurant. Her mother seemingly lost her way and literally took off in another direction. When the dreamer and the crowd arrived at the restaurant, they had to walk through a bedroom to get inside the restaurant. In the bed were actor John Goodman and his comedienne television wife Roseanne Barr. They smiled and wished everyone well as they went by.

DREAM 25B—INTERPRETATION

The dream started out by recognizing that she was composed of many different parts (the crowd she was leading) that needed to be nurtured (dining at a luxury restaurant.) Her mother introject was an irritant to her stability, as her mother was impulsive and stubborn in the face of her advanced age. She felt that her mother had frequently influenced her to go the wrong direction in life, which was exactly what her mother introject did in the dream.

This dream was giving her reassurance that she was on the right track in the sense of nurturing herself. This was represented by a famous couple who were married (marriage is a major symbol of integration since it represents actions integrating with emotions). The integration (the couple) is represented by positive actions (a Good Man) being intimate with beneficial emotions (comedienne actress Roseanne Barr).

The perfection of the symbolism was verified when the client emphasized that she felt like she was "acting" in new ways. It was taking her some getting used to the new behaviors. Dr. Carl Jung frequently pointed out that everything in a dream is "just so." There is no detail that is not important. The dream therapist is much more likely to under-interpret a dream than to over-interpret it.

DREAM 25C: ONLY DOPES USE DOPE

A 19-year-old man dreamt that he was at a banquet table in a palace in medieval times. He was eating a large and sumptuous meal. Suddenly men started injecting the food with drugs. The other people became silly and laughed stupidly.

DREAM 25C—INTERPRETATION

The dream announced that it was delivering an important and time-tested message with the extremely archetypal setting of a medieval palace. Medieval royalty is thoroughly ensconced deeply in the Western collective unconscious and shows up frequently in dreams. The men injecting the food with drugs were the drug addicted action parts of his psyche. The dreamer wanted to believe that the crystal meth he abused was nurturing for him. The other parts of his psyche begged to differ and emphasized that the crystal meth abuse was making him stupid.

SPECIAL NOTE ON EATING IN DREAMS

Eating food in dreams involves nurture; however, the objects eaten are not always food per se. In those cases, eating can be a sign that the dreamer is incorporating qualities of the eaten object into their personality/being. It can be a sign that a change that occurred based on past experience was now being fully incorporated (eaten) into the dreamer.

DREAM 25D: CONTAINING CHANGE

A 27-year-old woman had a dream about a year prior to the dream I will describe in which her sister, to whom she was very close, was arguing with her husband in a large and complex mansion. This dream is being mentioned because it gives guidelines regarding the emotional change the dreamer experienced.

In the first part of the current dream, she was in a beach house where there were numerous artists painting and displaying their works of art.

The dream shifted to her viewing a bird, a worm, and a snake. The snake and bird were in a struggle and the bird was doing the better of the two. The bird specifically pecked at and did damage to the snake's eyes. The worm was there, but was mostly uninvolved.

She then saw herself literally eating soft clay mugs used for drinking water. She enjoyed this experience and felt satisfied.

DREAM 25D—INTERPRETATION

The dream about her sister and brother-in-law arguing in a large and complex mansion, which she had a year prior to the current dream, was a good summary of the dreamer's psychological state one year prior to the more recent dream. A house can represent the dreamer to some extent because it is the framework from which the dreamer lives. The dream first asserted that the dreamer was a complex person, with many different parts (rooms) to her personality. The argument was representative of her emotions (her sister) being at war with her actions (her brother-in-law). The dreamer was psychiatrically hospitalized around that time.

A beach house is psychologically located between the subconscious (the water) and the conscious (the mainland). As such, it is where semiconscious impulses may become action. The numerous artists indicated that there were many creative parts of her. She had recently started painting and doing crafts.

Snakes represent change because they completely shed their skin. A bird takes flight and frequently is a symbol of freedom, with semi-spiritual overtones. The struggle between the bird and snake indicated that the parts of her that wanted more freedom were dominating more recently, as she was less timid in taking everyday risks (such as driving on the freeway). The worm was there because of the saying, "The early bird gets the worm." She noted that she always functioned better when she got up early in the morning.

The mugs in the dream were used to contain and administer water (emotions) to herself. One drinks water in a mostly controlled way, as drinking too fast or too much can create a mess. The mugs were made of soft clay, which relates to soft and earthy emotions. When one eats something or someone in a dream, it typically means that the dreamer is incorporating the qualities of the eaten object into their being/personality.

The dream was dramatizing the change she made in how she handled her emotions (water). She was now more able to contain and control her emotions and was able to release and dispense her emotions appropriately, so that her emotions became softer and more helpful/nurturing. The dream's climax was her incorporating significant creative and soft emotions in a properly controlled way that still allowed for appropriate and nourishing release of nurturing emotions. Her eating the soft mugs was making the ability to control and dispense emotion in a useful way a part of her.

Chapter 26:
Clothing Is Psychological
Body Armor in Dreams

Key 26: Clothing in dreams is virtually always representative of the dreamer's psychological defenses. Clothing is the surface or outside veneer that we present to the world. It has everything to do with how we want other people to see us, and much to do with how people actually do see us. It is the costume for the role we are playing at the time, whether that be worker, student, professional, athlete or man about town. The choices are unlimited and represent a reflection of what we want to project to the world and what we are able to project to the others, given the constraints of income or body features. In dreams, there are no constraints imposed by reality, so that we get a much more accurate reading of the dreamer's defenses.

Many dreams are about old defenses that resurface often at the dreamer's request. The dreamer may be looking through clothes in a closet or clothing store to either find defenses that worked in the past or new defenses that may fit the current situation better. Lack of clothing or nudity sends a powerful message. The dreamer is then typically conveying that he feels exposed and vulnerable in the situation.

DREAM 26A: INVESTING IN SOLUTIONS

A 26-year-old man dreamt that he was in a mall. He was both selling and buying clothing.

His colleague was a beautiful woman. Then he noticed a podium that was in the entry way of a restaurant. On the podium was a stack of blank paper with a large highlighter next to it.

DREAM 26A—INTERPRETATION

In my experience, when a dream starts out with a shopping mall, the dream is going to talk about or offer solutions to how one was mauled ("malled") in life. Many times the dream is referring to one's career or work life, as the dream occurs within a commercial establishment. Clothing almost invariably refers to the dreamer's defenses.

This was an early therapy dream, and the dreamer was deciding what defenses he would use. He was deciding which parts of therapy he would accept or "buy." He was also evaluating whether he would be able to "sell" changes he made to himself to other people.

The podium was at the entrance to a restaurant because the dream was trying to signal to the dreamer what would be nurturing to him. He wrote several books in the past, but hadn't written in two years because he was preoccupied with stress. The dream highlighted the importance of writing to his nurture and wellbeing by providing a stack of paper with a large highlighter (highlighting the importance of writing for him), which was on the way to a restaurant.

DREAM 26B: THE CHANGE WILL DO YOU GOOD

A 41-year-old woman dreamt that she had to take care of the baby of her emotionally disturbed friend while parties were occurring around them. The parties were celebrating all manner of events, including birthdays, anniversaries, and baby showers. And then the dream shifted to the inside of a ladies' bathroom. While she was using a stall, a "party girl" was urging her to join in one of the celebrations. She then saw herself cleaning up the messes left behind by all the parties. Then she and a multitude of other cleaners were changing their clothes. While she was changing, she noticed a tall, dark, handsome man smiling at her in the distance.

DREAM 26B—INTERPRETATION

The emotionally disturbed woman and all the characters in the dream are parts of the dreamer's psyche. The dream starts out by specifically pointing to a major problem in her life. That is, she turns to mothering to console her emotions rather than engaging in celebrations of life.

The bathroom is where we dispense of things we no longer need. Whatever immediately precedes the bathroom is usually connected with what needs to be eliminated from life. The dream was stating that she needed to quit turning to mothering her emotions and ignoring having active social fun. The "party girl" part of her wanted her to turn her emotions toward happy social functioning.

Clothing represents our defenses. Changing clothes in a dream means that your subconscious wants you to change the way you function. She exposed herself and made herself more vulnerable, so that the positive action part of herself (the **Heroic Masculine**) was attracted to the person she was becoming. The positive action part of herself wanted her to quit devoting all her energy to cleaning up other people's messes.

DREAM 26C: RUMMAGING THROUGH YOUR DEFENSES

A 42-year-old year old woman dreamt that she was in a house with her mother and sister, looking through an old closet. They were finding items to include in their garage sale. She looked through her old clothes and could not find an old pair of shoes she had worn when she was twenty. She went to the front yard of their home and found the pair of shoes. She was surprised that the shoes were actually included in the rummage sale. She packed the shoes away in a box and took them back to the house.

DREAM 26C—INTERPRETATION

Each character in the dream was a different part of her psyche. This dream announced that it was about her emotional functioning because all three characters were female. There was the mother introject, her ego self and her sister (who was really just a doubling of the dreamer herself, as a sister one year older was the closest representation of the woman that the dream could use). When a dream wants to emphasize something, it gives you two, and sometimes three of the same.

Carl Jung thought of clothes as metaphorically representing our defenses, since clothes are the barrier between ourselves and the outside world. Shoes are supportive defenses that help us get somewhere in life. The dream expresses alarm that she is "selling off" some of her old defenses commercially. She was working very hard to get a promotion. When asked what defenses she used when she was twenty, she indicated that she always did her work early in the day when she was younger. She noted that she also worked out when she was twenty, and she had gained a full shoe size since then, which she thought was due to her increased weight.

The dream was therefore recommending that she obtain more emotional support. She was introverted and was neglecting her social life too much. The dream also indirectly recommended that she work out to help her lose weight. After all, she gained a full shoe size due to her weight. She decided to heed the dream's advice to also complete her work early in the day so that she could reinforce herself more later in the day by doing what she really wanted to do.

DREAM 26D: BECAUSE OF YOU

A 28-year-old woman dreamt that she was going into her house and saw her old boyfriend delivering a couch to her home. He took the couch upstairs. She waved goodbye to him as he came down the stairs and left the house. She then found herself naked and looking into her car to see his mother and mentally retarded brother inside the car. She returned to her house and went upstairs to put on some clothes. She then went to her car and found just her stepsister in the passenger seat. As she drove away, she thought that it should have been her mother sitting next to her.

DREAM 26D—INTERPRETATION

The boyfriend in the dream was the boyfriend with whom she was first sexually involved. They had sex often, but the relationship ended after he ignored her wishes that she did not want to have sex on one occasion and he went ahead and raped her. She cried while he was doing it. He was delivering the "couch" in the dream because he was the reason she sought therapy, i.e., the "couch." She was now involved with a good man and was disturbed that occasionally, when he did something that reminded her of the old boyfriend, she became unresponsive sexually.

A house frequently represents the dreamer, and this especially seems to be the case with women. Different areas of the house correspond roughly to different areas of the body. Her old boyfriend was delivering the couch upstairs because the dream was recommending that she attend therapy to ease her mind (upstairs roughly signals the head or brain). Freud noted that climbing stairs often referred to intercourse because climbing steps is a rhythmic activity that ends in a climax.

Her being naked indicated that she felt exposed and vulnerable. His mother in the car is the emotionally supportive role she played for her boyfriend. His retarded brother is the part of her that had the sentiment, "I don't think he ever really realized what he did," by having sex with her against her wishes. She returned to the house to her upstairs (head or mind) to get some clothes. Clothing invariably represents the dreamer's defenses, as clothing is the face or armor we present to the world. She was now ready to go somewhere in life, represented by her getting in the driver's seat of her car, but did not feel that she was getting the support she needed. In the passenger seat was a similar- aged stepsister with whom she had never really got along instead of the emotionally supportive mother she felt she needed. To a certain extent, she was conflicted and fighting within herself over what happened instead of granting herself nurturing forgiveness.

SPECIAL NOTE ON SHOES AND LEGS

Shoes and legs have meanings especially relevant to therapy. Legs support us and get us somewhere in life on their own power. Shoes are the protective shield housing this personal supportive conveyance. The special supportive meaning of shoes was perhaps best illustrated by Dorothy's ruby slippers in "The Wizard of Oz." Dorothy returned to her emotionally supportive home by clicking her red ruby slippers together while saying, "There's no place like home."

DREAM 26E: DOWN THE RABBIT HOLE

A 36-year-old female dreamt that she was staring into a shoebox that had magical slippers in them. She put the shoes on and was magically transported to the headquarters of her bank, which was in another state on the West Coast.

Dream 26E—Interpretation

Shoes indicate support in getting somewhere with effort. The shoes protect and support your efforts to move forward in life. The dream indicated that she was getting support at work. She put on the shoes and was transported like "Alice in Wonderland" (or "The Wizard of Oz") down the rabbit hole to a new and magical place. She was just recently promoted to a supervisor position where she was given more support, with increased pay, prestige, and more workers to help her. It felt magical that she had broken the glass ceiling and joined the management of her bank, which tended to be very old school. It is perhaps significant that she was relocated to a more prestigious position on the West Coast. The good witch in "The Wizard of Oz" was the witch of the West, who is an example of the positive **Queen Archetype**.

Every detail in a dream means something.

Dream 26F: You Must Be Pulling My Leg

A 28-year-old man dreamt that he was in a dark hallway standing over the dead body of his older brother. All of a sudden, and to his surprise, the brother grabbed his leg. He was alive and well.

Dream 26F—Interpretation

His brother was a brave and athletic man with whom my client used to mountain climb. My client went to college (which none of his relatives did) and did well. His brother became a soldier and was the epitome of the **Heroic Masculine** whose motto is "To serve and protect."

The dreamer was fighting pancreatic cancer and had radiation and chemotherapy. He was assured that he had stage four cancer and had only two months to live. My client went on a series of adventures, such as mountain climbing, sky diving and complex roller coaster rides. His cancer miraculously went into remission. Deepak Chopra noted that when a person is exposed to scary and thrilling activities like a challenging roller coaster ride, the body produces many leukocytes, which fight cancer. The dreamer's "bucket list" of thrilling activities he wanted to do before he died may have saved his life.

The dream was reassuring him that his own **Heroic Masculine** was alive and vital and was there to support him (which is why his own **Heroic Masculine** grabbed his leg in the dream). Representation of legs frequently involves issues of internal support, i.e., having the gumption to move through life.

CHAPTER 27:
ALCOHOLISM

Key 27: Alcoholism is an attempt to get personal power from a bottle and many times to obliterate repetitive anxiety-producing memories.

Dr. Carl Jung, the master of dream interpretation, knew Bill, who wrote the Big Book for Alcoholics Anonymous. Jung once said to an alcoholic who was seeking psychotherapy words to the effect of "my art will not heal you." Jung thought the alcoholic was trying to get his spiritual or personal power from a bottle. That is why the twelve steps of Alcoholics Anonymous rely so heavily upon the concept of a higher power. The generic higher power, which is drawn from within to connect with the universe, replaces the addiction to alcohol. The mistake the alcoholic is making is trying to get his or her personal efficacy from a bottle.

On the Minnesota Multiphasic Personality Inventory, which was the standard for objective personality assessment for years, there is a scale called the MacAndrews Scale. Of its thirty-three or so items, only about three or four items deal directly with alcohol. The other items as a group seem to be keying on the person wanting to do something repetitive to forget their worries and to reduce anxiety. What is interesting about this scale is that it is good at measuring many different types of addiction, whether it be alcohol, drugs or an eating disorder. Dreams are good at helping the person discover their underlying anxiety that may be contributing to an addiction.

DREAM 27A: ROLLING IN THE DEEP

A 38-year-old woman dreamt she was approaching a beautiful home in a residential area that she always wanted to live in. She went into the house and found a walk-in closet. In the closet was another door, which led to another door, and so forth. The last of many doors went to a downward stairway.

She then dreamt that she had an affair with a male friend. This friend was different from her fiancé. The fiancé was strict and disciplined and thought mental health was mostly achieved by determination, which could be done by anyone. Her friend was empathic and was a sober alcoholic for the last eight years.

DREAM 27A—INTERPRETATION

She had this dream the night before her initial therapy session. The new house represented the new self she wanted to become. The closet frequently refers to secrets, such as skeletons in the closet or coming out of the closet. She went deeper within herself in the closet, which was what she wanted to do in therapy. The downward stairway led to the subconscious, the underlying reasons for her conflicts.

The woman was an alcoholic who had been sober for three years, but who had relapsed in the last three weeks. Her fiancé represented her strict, disciplined actions that allowed her to be sober for two years. The friend represented the positive action part of herself that was more accepting of the trials and tribulations of alcoholism. Her having sex with this part was an indication that she wanted to integrate with the positive healing part of herself that was empathic while being successful in overcoming alcoholism.

DREAM 27B: OBSTACLES AND NEEDED CHANGES

A 33-year-old woman dreamt that she was driving her car through the back alley of the neighborhood where she grew up. She had to make her way around the folded down mast of a sailboat. Further on, she had to make her way past a large bar with three large bar stools around it. She then saw, in an open area, a little girl running from an aggressive male German shepherd dog. To get away from the dog, the child ran into a wall covered with bushes and disappeared like Alice in Wonderland.

DREAM 27B—INTERPRETATION

A car frequently represents making our way through life. The back alley represented the **Shadow** and mostly secret events that occurred in her life. A sailboat navigates waters (emotions) under its own wind power. The sailboat in this case represented her belief that she could handle anything alone, which kept her from coming to psychotherapy much sooner. This belief was an obstacle to her getting better.

She had been in three major relationships and they were each decimated by alcoholism, which was represented by the large bar with the three huge bar stools. Dogs frequently go with male affection. This dog represented her experience of males from her father and her relationships that men were not affectionate and were aggressive. Her inner child, or little girl, tended to try to escape from her harsh relationship history by escaping within herself to a land of fantasy—like Alice in Wonderland, she escaped down the rabbit hole into her own world. She needed to go to therapy and face the fears within.

DREAM 27C: WHY I DROVE MYSELF TO RELAPSE

A 34-year-old woman dreamt that she was taken for a ride to a new house by her former husband and the woman with whom he had an affair. She went inside and found her good fireman boyfriend making a papaya smoothie for her. She took over the making of the smoothie and added alcohol. She then saw herself at a house where she was planning to live with her new boyfriend. The house also contained two of his previous relationships, and she could not abide allowing these women to live in the same house with her.

DREAM 27C—INTERPRETATION

The dream started by talking about how she was "taken for a ride" by her former husband's betrayal. Betrayal drove her to drink (remember that each character in the dream is a part of the dreamer herself). Her current boyfriend was the embodiment of the **Heroic Masculine**. She did not allow being nurtured by the masculine because of previous abuse, which included being raped as an adult and being emotionally mistreated by her father. She wanted to nurture herself preferentially but did not know how to do it without including alcohol to cover her pain. Intrapsychically, she did not have an actively evolved **Heroic Masculine** within herself that knew how to properly nourish her. This is the hardest part of dream interpretation—to fully recognize that each character in the dream is a part of herself, with females going more with emotions and men going more with actions. Interpersonally, her boyfriend frequently complained that she would not accept support/nurture from him.

In the last scene, the dream shifted to pointing to additional problems in the relationship. Remember that a house can represent the dreamer herself to some extent because it was the framework out of which she lived. There were emotional scars within herself from previous relationships (the two women). Interpersonally, she wondered how much she was being compared to her boyfriend's previous girlfriends.

DREAM 27D: YOU HAVE WHAT IT TAKES, BABY

A 33-year-old man was at a party with his paternal cousin who was the son of his father's brother. (This cousin had serious drinking problems and was recently arrested for DWI.) He then saw himself as a baby boy, with blonde hair and blue eyes, who was falling down everywhere he went. He saw this baby crawling along the beach in a rocky area where the baby was in danger. He then saw himself having the choice of three beautiful women seated at a table.

DREAM 27D—INTERPRETATION

He was having trouble with drinking too much and letting his anger out, which was destroying his marriage. His father drank excessively and was distant from the dreamer when he was a child. The dreamer and his father recently became closer by drinking together, which made his drinking problem worse. The dream announced at the beginning that it was going to be about his drinking problems. The baby was an archetype of his hopes and aspirations, which Dr. Carl Jung called the **Divine Child Archetype**. The **Divine Child** was a boy in this instance because the dream was focusing on his actions. He was ineffectual and clumsy, and he was hurting himself by drinking excessively, which was putting his life in danger. The dream ended by reassuring him that he had plenty of pleasant emotional resources (three beautiful women) from which to emotionally change himself (three signals change).

CHAPTER 28:
DRUGS

Key 28: Drugs are an attempt, at the best, to make one less aware of or to enhance reality. At the worst, drugs are an attempt to obliterate reality. The dreamer ends up trying to solve problems by going to a world that does not exist.

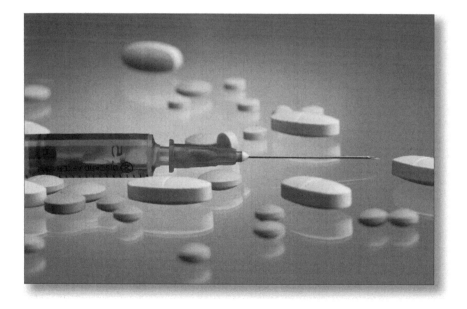

DREAM 28A: QUIETING THE TRUMPETING ELEPHANTS

A 29-year-old male dreamt that he was being chased by a herd of wild trumpeting elephants through his house. He ran upstairs and went to the second story balcony. He was forced to jump by the onslaught of elephants.

Then the dreamer found himself at the top of a high diving board. He dove into the pool, which turned into concrete as he was descending. He lay there, unconscious and paralyzed from the neck down.

The dream then changed to him being in the kitchen. His sister, who was a confidant and was one year younger, was also in the kitchen. His father was in the background. He dreamt that there was a partially filled bag of marijuana on the table. He picked it up, hoping that his father had not yet noticed. He ran outside and down the street for a couple of blocks and then threw the bag in some bushes.

Dream 28A—Interpretation

A house to some extent, particularly if it is the family home, can represent the dreamer himself. Wild animals represent instinctive energy. He was full of instinctive energy, which terrified him. The house often corresponds to the dreamer anatomically. His running upstairs (to his brain) during the daytime indicated that his conscious awareness of the huge charging energy within him scared him so that he would do almost anything to get away from it. He "damped down" his energy and awareness with marijuana. He descended (dived) into a world of hurt, where he lost support (legs support us and get us around, and he severely damaged these abilities). It also was a condensation since he also lost emotional support from others.

He was taking risks with drugs, hoping to plumb his emotions (water is almost invariably emotion, and a pool represents manmade and controlled emotions). His attempts to use drugs were misguided and harmful, as abusing drugs was simply trying a concrete solution (the pool turned into concrete) to emotional problems. He ended up being stymied and defeated.

The last part of the dream involved the kitchen, which is a place of creativity. His sister represented supportive emotions. His father introject, which focuses on his action decisions, was in the background. He decided that he needed to get the motivation-robbing marijuana out of his life, especially because it was affecting his creativity.

His dad would be proud of him.

DREAM 28B: NOT BAD, OLD MAN!

A 29-year-old man dreamt that he was a passenger in a car driven by a high school friend with whom he used to abuse substances. He was cheating the substance abuser out of money and wondered why he did not feel guilty about it. He then dreamt that he was with his successful grandfather. They were running up a hill in a race to get to the top. They arrived simultaneously at the top of the hill. The dreamer slapped his grandfather fondly on the back and said, "Not bad, old man!"

DREAM 28B—INTERPRETATION

He wondered about starting college, as he could do the academic work but admittedly was having trouble with motivating himself because of the feeling that he was starting to get old. Years of marijuana abuse had literally robbed him of motivation. The substance abusing driver was the part of himself that wasted his energy on marijuana, which he smoked every day back then. His grandfather was a successful former Marine who went on to become a semi-famous scientist. That he was cheating the substance abuser out of money meant that he decided not to expend his energy (money) on idle time wasted on marijuana. The race with the successful grandfather up a hill was reassurance that he was not too old to achieve major goals in life. He had a potentially successful part of himself ready to persevere against adverse conditions (the hill).

Dream 28C: Life Is Just a Bowl of Candy

A 19-year-old woman dreamt that she, her sister, and two friends were eating candy that was actually LSD. She was then at a party, where a friend who betrayed her many times was being insulted by three guests. Her friend was completely unaware that she was being insulted. Her friend then went to a pool where there was a water slide, and she went down it, even though it did not look safe. My client, nevertheless, went down the same water slide. When she hit the water, she was in the middle of the ocean. She tried to swim to a nearby boat that was badly damaged. She made it to the boat and realized she had to repair it.

DREAM 28C—INTERPRETATION

The sister in this dream is actually a doubling of the dreamer herself. When a dream wants to emphasize something, it gives you two. Her sister was the closest person to the dreamer herself. The dream started by announcing that there were times when the dreamer thought she was being sweet (candy), but she was actually deluding herself (LSD). That her sister whom she loved, along with her friends, were also deluding themselves meant that a large part of her was distorting reality. She could not recognize when she was being mistreated. Her friend at the party represented the naive part of her that followed untrustworthy people. She followed a part of herself that did not even know when she was being insulted. She ended up sliding and plunging into the ocean. The dream was giving her a wakeup call that she needed to immerse herself

in her emotions (the water). She had to navigate her way to a boat that needed repair. The dream was screaming that she needed to change herself and navigate the oceans (her subconscious emotions) differently.

DREAM 28D: WAITING ON THE ZOMBIES

A 26-year-old man dreamt that he was riding a bicycle in a valley and was going up a series of mountains, one after another. Each time he crested a hill, he could see a person in the distance. He went down into the next valley and crested the next hill and saw the same person, but each time the person was at the same distance from him and he got no closer to his goal. The dream then shifted to medieval times, where he was fighting a battle without armor. He kept fighting, but every so often he was blindsided and knocked to the ground. He would get up and keep fighting.

Then the dream shifted and he was being chased by zombies. He made it to his car, where he felt safe. Suddenly, green goop invaded the car and squeezed its way inside. It took the form of a phony green female.

DREAM 28D—IN-TERPRETATION

In Greek myths, Sisyphus was condemned to eternally roll a boulder up a mountain, which always rolled back down the mountain right before he reached the top. Then he performed the whole process over and over again for eternity. This dream used the **Sisyphus Archetype**. The dream indicated that he was working hard (climbing mountains) and trying to balance himself (the bicycle) and achieve, but that brought him no closer to people.

The medieval battle was very archetypal, indicating that a major conflict for the dreamer was that he did not protect himself enough (did not wear armor), and often was blindsided by interpersonal conflict. He was very conflicted about using the **Savage Masculine** when necessary to defend himself. The last part explained why he overused marijuana. The zombies were depressed parts of him that were like the living dead zombies. He was trying to escape depression, but received nothing but a phony emotional good feeling from the marijuana that got him nowhere, as the car did not move in spite of the impending zombies. It was time to move. It was not time to sit back, enjoy a joint, and wait for the zombies.

DREAM 28E: FIDDLING WHILE ROME IS BURNING

A 38-year-old woman dreamt that her husband went to a nearby house with a drug abusing and drug injecting woman. Her husband was smoking marijuana like there was no tomorrow. She saw herself going to the neighbors' house next door and asking them why they did not do something about her husband and the woman. The neighbors responded that they were busy having a barbeque picnic.

DREAM 28E—INTERPRETATION

The dreamer had years of abusing hard drugs before she was married. She and her husband were in marital therapy because of recent stress. Her husband never abused substances. In the dream, he represented her action self, the part that decides what to do. She was concerned that she was unconsciously being untrue to herself by having cravings for drug abuse. The dreamer is worried that she will be "unfaithful" to her emotions by acting on the cravings.

Her going to a nearby neighbor's house indicated that her emotional self, which is typically represented in dreams as a female, was trying to alert other parts of the psyche that something needed to be done about this possible breach of faith in giving up her sobriety. The other parts indicated that they were busy with a barbeque, which uses fire. This is another way for the other parts of her psyche to say that they are busy nurturing (the barbeque food) themselves for the changes (fire used to barbeque) they have made. Her emotional self is appalled that the other parts of her psyche are fiddling while Rome is burning. Do they not know that life is no picnic?

CHAPTER 29:
THANKS FREUD

Key 29: There are some images that Freud interpreted so startlingly clearly that it behooves the dream interpreter to pay special attention to these images, because they are frequently on the mark.

This is not to say that Freud was right on everything, but I have found the following images to be frequent and recurrent because they refer to common events.

DREAM 29A: STAIRWAY TO HEAVEN

A 33-year-old woman dreamt that she was in a two-story condominium. She, her roommate and her husband were looking from the upper floor down the stairway. There was witchcraft in the air and a broom floated up near the ceiling of the first floor and was banging rhythmically against the ceiling. She noted that when she went to look at the broom, it floated down somewhat and became horizontal and then sprang up to a 45° angle, which surprised and fascinated her.

DREAM 29A—INTERPRETATION

The condominium in the dream is like a condominium that she lived in with a female roommate who was very sexual and manipulative with men. Movement down or looking down a staircase reflects moving into the subconscious. Freud related the image of a staircase to having sex since you climb it rhythmically and reach a climax at the top. If a stairway is featured in a dream, sexual issues are nearby. The broom is associated with witchcraft

(a **Shadow** side of sex; sex can be quite magical). The broom is an obvious phallic symbol with its rhythmic banging and its springing up due to an erection. The dream, more or less, is recommending that she have sex with her husband.

DREAM 29B: THE SOUND AND THE FURY

A 19-year-old man dreamt that he was on his father's farm. His father was yelling at him and telling him that he wasn't doing something right. He had a favorite aunt and uncle who also lived on the farm in a separate house who were good people, but who were naive and apologetic for his father's abuse. There was also a hardworking black man who was working with the dreamer. He saw a large tornado heading for the farm. He was having a sexual relationship with a woman of whom his father disapproved. There were two gigantic turbines turning in the opposite way the tornado was swirling so that it prevented the full force of the tornado from developing.

DREAM 29B—INTERPRETATION

He grew up on a farm. His father beat and abused him several times. The aunt and the uncle represented expected family emotion and action, which he accepted as a little boy. He made excuses for his father's abuse as a naive child. In the dream the father represented the part of the father introject that was associated with self-abuse (each character in the dream is a part of the dreamer's psyche). The aunt and uncle represented the little boy part of himself that wanted to make excuses for his father's behavior to some extent. The hardworking black man was representative of a more heroic and soulful action part of himself, his **Heroic Masculine** (which was the part that was in love with the woman). He felt conflicted about the relationship because it was with a somewhat older woman with whom a former friend had been involved in the past.

The huge tornado represented the powerful instinctive forces within himself that were confused and chaotic. Tornadoes, typhoons and hurricanes often represent feelings of conflict and chaos over sexual issues. Like sex and love, a tornado is a powerful natural force that you do not have total control over, which can affect your life and living arrangements significantly. He was torn between his love for the woman and some residual feelings of guilt. The gigantic turbines were representative of machinations (rationalizations) within himself that he consciously and purposefully developed to reduce self-abusive thinking and guilt from the past that would interfere with his love.

PREFACE TO DREAM 29C: SUPEREGO FIGURES

Freud talked extensively about the id, the ego, and the superego. A dream almost always has an id feature, as managing basic instincts is one of the main jobs of the executive ego. Superego figures are those figures that uphold societal rules. This can involve parental figures to some extent, but superego figures are usually figures that directly enforce the law of the land, such as police, state troopers, and FBI. Sometimes an overly harsh superego will be represented by an unusual and graphic figure, such as in Dream 29C.

DREAM 29C: CUT IT OUT

A 28-year-old man dreamt that he was with a girl of less than average appearance. Suddenly a butcher ran after them, throwing butcher knives. The dreamer saw himself finally beating the butcher with his fists.

DREAM 29C—INTERPRETATION

The dreamer was recently worried that he may have contracted a sexually transmitted disease from a girl with a bad reputation after having sex with her when he was intoxicated. The butcher was the harsh part of his superego, which was castigating him. He internally was condemning himself obsessively, although there was no sign that he had an STD. His continuing health in this regard was confirmed by a doctor and medical tests. The dream was graphically threatening him that "sleeping with any old piece of meat" (his words) had to stop. It was concretely telling him to "cut out" such behavior. His obsessions of rethinking this incident over and over needed to stop, which is why the dream ended with his beating the overly harsh superego, the butcher, into submission.

DREAM 29D: NOT AS MUCH FUN AS I THOUGHT

A 38-year-old woman dreamt that she was on a roller coaster surrounded by very vivid lights of all colors. Her husband refused to go on the ride with her. When she got off the roller coaster ride, he was puzzled and confused about how much she enjoyed the ride. They somehow found out, to her horror, that she was artificially inseminated during the roller coaster ride.

DREAM 29D—INTERPRETATION

A roller coaster can represent manmade sexual thrills since it is constructed by men, involves a lot of up and down thrills, and can be scary. When talking about sexual matters, the emphasis is on the entertainment and "fun" of sex. These associations exist because a roller coaster is part of an amusement park.

Her daughter had been molested for some months by an older cousin. She thought things were going well, and she was having fun at her job. She was unaware of the molestation of her daughter and was also unaware that her husband was failing at his job. She had sexual difficulties after finding out about the molestation. Finding out about her husband hiding his work troubles only made sexual functioning more difficult for her. The dream was about being unable to share the "fun" and excitement of sex due to the horror she felt about being screwed over when she thought she was having fun.

Her puzzlement and confusion was making it difficult to actively enjoy sex. Her husband in this dream is a condensation because he represented her love life actions and also, on the interpersonal level, was representing himself and his contribution to her sexual difficulties. The vivid multicolored lights indicated that intense emotions were involved.

PREFACE TO DREAM 29E: NOT ALWAYS SEXUAL

Roller coasters are a good example where the Freudian interpretation frequently holds, but such is not always the case. Dream 29E is a good example that shows that the interpretation can sometimes be completely devoid of sexual reference. Sorry Sigmund, not everything is sex.

DREAM 29E: LIFE IS SCREWY

A 47-year-old man dreamt that he was riding in a roller coaster that went upward in a quick, twisting corkscrew pattern. He arrived at the top, where the ride ended and his roller coaster car was upside down. He had a safety harness on. People at the top helped him safely disembark from the roller coaster ride.

DREAM 29E—INTERPRETATION

He was "upside down" on his home equity and could not make the mortgage payments. He scrambled to find resources to help him out of his dilemma, which involved friends, the church and the government (many people "at the top"). Various people and agencies helped him with payments until he got rid of the house. He finally bought a foreclosed property, which went up in value a full fifty percent in one year. It was a screwy and dizzying experience that led him to safety with the help of people at the top, even though he previously was "upside down" financially. In going through this whole process, this independent man frequently had to convince himself to let other people help him if he wanted to emerge from the financial bind he was in.

PREFACE TO DREAM 29F: SOMETIMES A CIGAR IS JUST A CIGAR

Sometimes a purely Freudian interpretation can be so wedded to the sexual motivations that it strains credibility. Dream 29F is a good example, where the more common and colloquial meaning seems to be more useful.

DREAM 29F: JUST DO IT

A 26-year-old woman dreamt that she and her father were standing next to a closed casket. Her sister was to her left on the other side of the casket. Her sister reached up and pulled out one of her own front teeth.

DREAM 29F—INTERPRETATION

This woman was depressed and passive and had extreme difficulty getting herself to accomplish tasks. Her father in the dream is her father introject, which typically focuses upon action. Her sister was very active, extroverted and social. The closed casket implies that she was losing a part of herself, as death in a dream can mean that a part of the person's psyche was diminished.

The sister losing her tooth indicated that she felt that she lost her effectiveness, that this active and more social part of her psyche represented by her sister was losing its edge. Losing a tooth in a dream virtually guarantees the dreamer is feeling some form of a personal loss. The dreamer felt that she was losing her bite. A good father introject typically encourages action. She was being warned of the consequences of inaction. The woman decided to engage in more social activities, which helped her to be less depressed.

To give you the contrasting and archaic classic Freudian interpretation, losing a tooth for a woman meant she wanted to have a 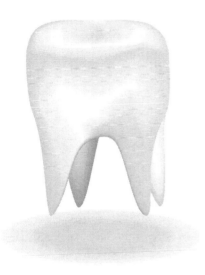 baby (because the tooth fell out of her body like a child is a part of her body before falling out, i.e., being born). For a man, losing a tooth supposedly had to do with masturbation. In the case of men, losing a tooth (a white substance) was being used by the dream as a metaphor for ejaculating semen. Considerable cognitive flexibility is needed to fully accept that metaphor.

CHAPTER 30:
HEALING

Key 30: When a dream uses a hospital or medical facility as the setting, it usually is dealing with healing. Animas, beautiful women, are frequently a sign of positive emotions, which can be the result or cause of healing, usually emotionally, but can refer to physical healing at times.

When the dreamer is either traveling to or in a medical setting, the dream is usually using the hospital or clinic as a metaphor to instruct the dreamer on how to heal herself. In archetypal healing dreams, the medical personnel may be medicine men or various sorts of herbal, intuitive and/or natural healers. The doctor or nurse, if male, is usually delivering messages regarding the action the dreamer needs to take to be healed. If the medical professional

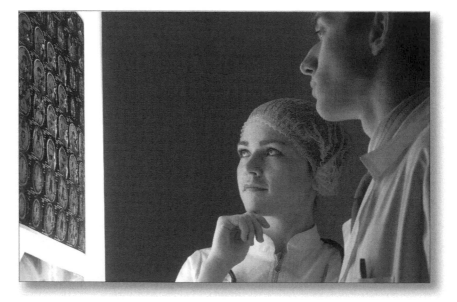

is female, it is more likely to be discussing corrective emotional healing. The dream uses the male/female dichotomy as code to distinguish action (male) suggestions from emotional (female) guidance in this area, as in many areas.

Beautiful women most often signal positive emotions, which can be the result or cause of the dreamer's healing. They frequently have blonde hair and blue eyes, as these physical characteristics are associated with the **Divine Child Archetype**, which essentially represents our hopes and dreams for the future. It should be pointed out that there is a special and **Archetypal Anima**, which is powerful indication that emotional healing is taking place. In classic art, notably that of Rembrandt, the attractive women are frequently women with light brown and softly curling hair. These **Animas** are ingrained in the collective unconscious as archetypes of beauty because of the classic paintings by artists such as Rembrandt.

DREAM 30A: A GLUTTON FOR PUNISHMENT

A 44-year-old man dreamt that he went to a hospital that was located near where he grew up. There were two nurses who escorted him to treatment. Instead of walking into a treatment room, they walked into a time warp that took them back to the past. He knew he could go anywhere in the past and correct past actions.

He came upon a morbidly obese woman with blonde hair and blue eyes who was talking. He came up behind her with a gun and shot her. The woman was unharmed and simply kept talking. He saw a dark shadow profile of a man. He shot the man and felt relieved.

DREAM 30A—INTERPRETATION

He was severely physically abused as a child. He would hold in his feelings so that he did not give the abuser any indication how deeply the abuse hurt physically. When he grew up, he found that he tended to withhold emotions. When he did express emotions, too much anger escaped into the relationship.

His approaching the hospital meant that he was going to treatment, to therapy in this case. The two female nurses indicated that primarily his emotions needed treatment. The fact that there were two nurses suggested relationship issues were probably involved (it takes two people to form a relationship, an emotional relationship in this case).

The dream specified that he needed to change emotions (the woman he shoots). She had blonde hair and blue eyes, which are features of the **Divine Child** in Caucasian culture. His hopes and dreams were obviously frustrated as an abused child. His shooting her meant that he no longer wanted the frustrations to be part of his emotional makeup in relationships. Her being unhurt and grossly overweight signaled two things: (1) this part of his emotions would be hard for him to change, and (2) this part of his psyche made him a glutton for punishment (her being morbidly overweight). The **Shadow** man he shot was an embodiment of his angry actions, an excessively angry **Shadow**, which ended relationships. He went through a time in therapy where it was actually easier to control and limit angry actions, even though he still felt the anger inside. He definitely went through having "to fake it until he made it."

DREAM 30B: ANIMAS GIVING THE SAVAGE MASCULINE WHAT-FOR

A 36-year-old man dreamt that he was in his hometown Lutheran Church. His family and his abusive brother had their backs to the dreamer. The abusive brother handed a note to the dreamer, denying any abuse ever occurred. The dreamer knew that the abuser's view of events was in complete agreement with his mother's opinion. The dreamer responded with a note that the dreamer personally handed the abusive brother, detailing the truth of the abuse. A chorus of **Animas**, three attractive women at the front of the church, then sang the "truth" to the abuser in a jazzy rabble-rousing Chicago style. One **Anima** with brown and loosely curly Rembrandt-style hair was really into it. She sang in his face as loudly and insultingly as she possibly could.

DREAM 30B—INTERPRETATION

The man was beaten as a child on almost a weekly basis by a brother who was ten years older. The mother knew what was going on, but was complicit with the beatings because the victim reminded her of her husband, whom she despised. The victim had been in therapy for some time. He made a breakthrough when he wrote letters to the abuser that described the situation. The man made sure to mention that he forgave the abuser simply because he wanted to reclaim energy for his life that he previously had wasted on hating the abuser. The only reason the dreamer forgave him was for the dreamer's benefit. It is significant that he had three sisters (who were the three **Animas** in the dream) who cushioned and ameliorated the negative effects of the abuse by the **Savage Masculine** brother.

DREAM 30C: MY BETTER HALF

A 56-year-old man dreamt that he entered a Greek bathing/sauna/pool area surrounded by a multitude of artists painting. In the pool was an athletic man who looked like a Greek god. There was also an unbelievably beautiful woman swimming in the pool that slowly got out of the pool and walked toward his table. She sat down directly across from him at the table and they stared intensely into each other's eyes. She was transformed into being him, which alternated with him being her. He felt that she was eventually absorbed by and became a part of him, which was followed by a peaceful and calm feeling.

DREAM 30C—INTERPRETATION

The man was a writer who had recently struggled with being creative. He always felt unattractive and recently was worried about a relationship with a female friend. She thought of him only as a friend, while he entertained deeper feelings for her. He felt somewhat rejected, although that certainly was not her intent, by her deciding to actively date other men after a recent divorce.

The dream started out by reassuring him that he had many creative parts (the artists) of his psyche. The male Greek god in the water (emotions) was reassurance of his essential male psychological makeup. The seductive Greek goddess, an **Aphrodite Archetype**, was reassurance that he had beautiful emotions that were a part of him. The peace he felt was from all the reassurances at almost every level which was delivered mainly by the beautiful **Anima** goddess.

DREAM 30D: STOP PAYING FOR IT AND JOIN THE PARTY

A 27-year-old man dreamt that he went to see a prostitute. They talked awhile without anything happening, and then she told him she had to leave. He then went next door, where there was a party with drinking. A man and a lady were playing acoustic guitars. He thought the scene looked quite inviting. In fact, he found that the prostitute was at the party, as well. Then a beautiful woman walked up to him and told him he had to leave before he became too clingy and dependent.

DREAM 30D—INTERPRETATION

He recently decided that there were limits as to how involved he would become in relationships because in the past he had become too dependent. He was also trying to stay sober because he had abused drugs in the past. He wanted relationships that were simple and transparent.

The prostitute represented the part of him that wanted to be more businesslike in relationships. He avoided social interactions even though, before drugs became a problem, he was quite extroverted. He was worried about maintaining his sobriety and wanted to be less clingy in relationships.

The beautiful woman was an **Anima** figure, which represented the positive part of his emotions wanting him to change his attitude before allowing himself to "join the party." He tended either to become high and lean on a woman for support, or he withdrew and isolated himself. Dr. Carl Jung spoke of "holding the tension of the opposites." In many situations, such as this one, there was a tendency for him either to withdraw or to become dependent and high. He would swing from one opposite to the other. Jung pointed out that doing something in the middle was holding the tension of the opposites. It is usually more difficult to do, but a solution in the middle usually comes closest to being correct.

Staying with one all-or-nothing position felt safer, although it was ultimately less adaptive. The dream was saying that it was time for him to do something in the middle, to hold the tension of the opposites, by joining the party without becoming high and dependent. His problems with addiction stemmed partially from ingrained tendencies to become dependent in an attempt to overcome anxieties.

CHAPTER 31:
BIRTH AND DEATH

Key 31: Pregnancy and birth in a dream represent a new character being introduced to the dream, which is a signal that the dreamer is giving birth to a new part of himself. Death in a dream means that the dreamer has essentially changed or eliminated a part of her psyche. Sometimes death can be symbolic of a significant part of the psyche changing because of the actual-in-reality-death of a significant person such as a parent.

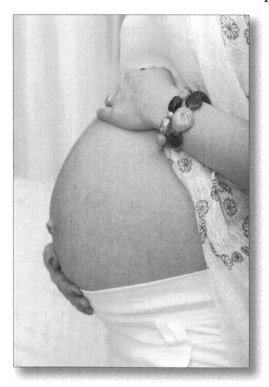

DREAM 31A: GROW MY ALIEN

A 28-year-old man dreamt that he had an alien baby attached to his hip. He wanted his girlfriend to sprinkle water over the baby so that it would grow.

DREAM 31A—INTERPRETATION

His fiancé was pregnant and they were planning to get married while he was getting a new job to support them. The baby was a part of him that was acting very different from how he behaved in the past. He now had goals and things that he wanted to accomplish. He was motivated. This was a brand new part of himself, which was so new that it felt alien. Water is almost invariably emotions. The dream was simply saying that he felt his girlfriend's support might help him grow into his new role of helping to take care of the baby.

DREAM 31B: FATHER LOVE

A 22-year-old college student dreamt that he was a pulmonary doctor who applied a defibrillator to his father's heart over and over, with great waves of electric energy, in a vain attempt to save his father's life.

DREAM 31B—INTERPRETATION

He was very close to his father. His father recently died from pulmonary embolism. Each character in the dream is a part of the dreamer's psyche. As such, the dream was giving some direction as to how the dreamer might try to heal himself. It was a condensation of the fact that he loved his father with all his heart, as the heart is the symbolic center of love. The father in the dream is the dreamer's own father introject. The dream was saying that he needed to revive the emotion of love to heal himself of the loss of his father. He recently was reconciling with a woman for whom he had electrifying love. He thought focusing on his love for this woman might help him emotionally.

DREAM 31C: THE FATHER PART OF ME NEEDS TO DIE

A 32-year-old man dreamt that he was in the house where he grew up. He was carrying the urn that contained his father's ashes. There was an old high school friend who was extroverted, friendly and manipulative whom he suspected of killing his father. He went into his backyard and found a recently covered grave. He dug up the soft earth and found many items that he did not want, such as beer of suspect quality, couch cushions and a loudspeaker. He decided to throw the items back into the grave and covered it. He felt relieved.

DREAM 31C—INTERPRETATION

When you dream of the house you grew up in, you are most often recontacting and examining the framework out of which you grew. His father was a large, arrogant alcoholic and physically abusive man who worked and then came home to watch television for long hours in true couch potato fashion. He drank a lot of alcohol during his viewing. His main contact with the family was to bark insults (the loudspeaker) or hit the dreamer for a transgression that existed only in his father's mind. Although he was a man of meager accomplishments, his father was a legend in his own mind.

The high school friend represented the **Trickster** part of the dreamer. The **Trickster** typically makes impossible situations work. It was no longer possible for the dreamer to retain his father's drinking and criticism habits. The dreamer's main relationship was in danger because he was drinking alone and becoming more depressed, which had its origin in his father's abuse of the dreamer.

The dream was recommending that he get rid of the remnants of his father that he still retained within himself. According to the dream, these introverted and depressed parts would best be replaced by a **Trickster's** sociability and extroversion. The remnants are like ashes—they are the residue left within the dreamer from his father. Cremation involves fire, which typically means transformation. The dreamer needed to avoid becoming a couch potato, drinking and loud behavior, which were represented by the father items he found in the grave. Those residual negative parts needed to stay buried.

CHAPTER 32:
NUMBERS

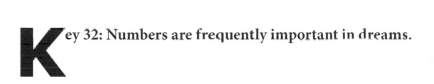

Key 32: Numbers are frequently important in dreams.

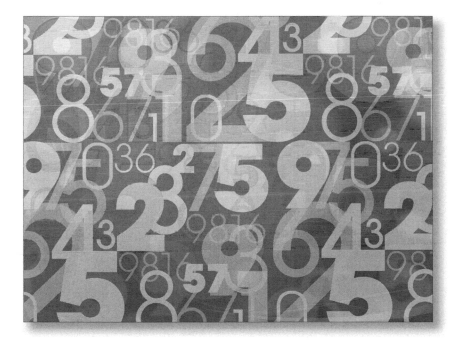

Numbers can have idiosyncratic meanings for the dreamer. The number may be a phone number, room number, address, or an amount of money recently spent. The interpreter will have to rely on the dreamer's associations to the number many times. It is important to ask, "Does the number show up anywhere in your life?"

I have come to an understanding of numbers that frequently show up in dreams. I have, with the help of others, come to see certain numbers as having special meaning. The single digit numbers usually have a somewhat standard meaning, with some numbers being more significant than others. There are common longer numbers that have strong associations, and these frequent fliers will be discussed in more detail. Here are the subconscious meanings the author frequently found clients have assigned to numbers:

◻ (0) Zero is a small circle. A circle is a symbol of the soul because it has no beginning and no end. Zero can also represent the cosmic void from which all creation proceeds.

◻ (1) One refers to the dreamer herself. The dreamer is the one.

◻ (2) Two frequently refers to a couple or a relationship between two people. When the dream wants to emphasize a point, it gives a dreamer signs such as two dogs, two females, or two males. Sometimes the dream will double the dreamer himself by including a best friend of the same age or a sibling close in age who has been emotionally close to the dreamer.

◻ (3) Three is by far the most useful number in helping to extract the meaning of a dream. Three is unstable and portends change because three people in a relationship are very unstable. Something is going to change. All good dramas have three major characters: the persecutor, the victim, and the rescuer. It is the pressure of change that is the fulcrum, and change drives the drama. The change can be dramatic. As with the number two, the dream will often triple characters (three females, three males, or three dogs) to underscore the meaning intended for the dreamer.

◻ (4) Four is my second favorite number in helping to discern the meaning of a dream. In contrast to unstable three, four is the number of stability. Four roommates are much more likely to reach a homeostasis or equilibrium than three roommates. There are four directions, four seasons, and four quarters to a football game. People from the four corners of the earth meet to constitute a whole functioning organization.

◻ (5) Five is most often meaningful if it is seen as four plus one. A new element is usually being introduced to a stable situation.

▫ (6) Six is often seen as two times three, which can mean that a couple or pair of people have to change. It can also be calling on the dreamer to make two changes (2 x 3 = 6).

▫ (7) Seven is most often the number signifying luck.

▫ (8) Eight is a very stable situation (2 x 4 = 8).

▫ (9) Nine is screaming for change (3 x 3 = 9).

▫ (12) I am compelled to mention the number twelve. Carolyn Myss, a medical intuitive who is steeped in Jungian dream interpretation, notes that twelve is a number of completion. It certainly is important in our culture, as there are twelve months in a year, twelve disciples with Jesus Christ, twelve items in a dozen, twelve tribes of Israel, and so forth.

▫ (13)Thirteen is the classic number of bad luck, so much so that buildings frequently do not have a thirteenth floor. An interpreter can often deconstruct longer numbers by viewing the number as a combination of the above elementary numbers and their associated meanings.

▫ A number mentioned in a dream can often refer to the age when the dreamer previously dealt with a conflict that was highly similar to the current situation or conflict in the dreamer's current life scenario.

▫ Addresses, room numbers, dates, exact sums of money, exact times of day, and the number of people in a group are frequently the subconscious source of an idiosyncratic number.

DREAM 32A: TAKE CARE OF YOURSELF ALREADY

A 46-year-old woman dreamt that she was on her daily walk when an exhausted 20-year- old girl slowly ran into her, and the woman helped ease the young woman's slow motion fall to the sidewalk. The young woman then had a miscarriage and was losing blood. The dreamer told someone to phone 911, and then saw herself as a doctor barking orders to medics to save the girl.

DREAM 32A—INTERPRETATION

Giving birth in a dream means that she was trying to give birth to a new part of herself. She was not ready for the new part, so she miscarried. She was trying to give birth to a part of herself that would work even harder, but that was not in the cards for her due to her health. Her inner physician took command and demanded that she take care of herself rather than add more work to her life.

Dr. Carl Jung was very much into numbers. Three is the number of change since three people is the most unstable number of people to have in a relationship, because two will ally more and one is always on the outside. Three times three is nine. The dream is emphasizing the need for change by squaring three. The 1's refer to the dreamer herself and two ones are given to emphasize the need is to change the dreamer herself. Both by situation and numerically, the dream is screaming that she needs to change by taking care of herself.

DREAM 32B: THE COST OF CHANGE

A 56-year-old woman dreamt that she was in the house where she grew up, but the house was barren and had no furniture. Her mother was showing her around. They went back to a room, which she thought was her bedroom. When they opened the door to the room, they felt a blast of air that cooled her down. She was shown that her bed would not be the king size bed that she slept on until recently. Her bed now would be half the size of a twin bed. The rest of the house was now full of beds of various sizes and shapes, as many people were going to live in the house now.

The dream shifted to her being with a female who was hired to give her a massage. The woman told the dreamer that it would be $360 for a ten-minute massage.

DREAM 32B—INTERPRETATION

The woman recently moved from a large and sumptuous house, where she lived alone, to her daughter's house. She had a relatively small room with a smaller bed. Her daughter and her husband had two active, elementary school girls. She liked living with her daughter in some ways, but missed her previous residence.

In the dream, her mother introject was exploring her deep-seated feelings about where she slept. The house in the dream was the house she lived in as a child, but it did not feel like home. The dream was indicating her subconscious feelings about living in her daughter's home.

Her daughter's home was supposed to be her home now, but it did not feel like home to her. There was something missing (the furniture). She, in fact, was having a fan blow air directly to her face all night long to calm her to sleep. The blast of air she felt in the dream literally meant to the dreamer that she did not like the atmosphere of the house.

The multiple beds indicated that there were too many people there for a woman who previously slept alone. She now felt crowded and had to share with others (the twin bed), which she was not used to. More than anything, her bed now did not feel like one she had made her own. She had not yet bonded with her daughter's home.

In the last part of the dream ($360 for a ten-minute massage), her subconscious is screaming that she felt that she could not afford to relax. Although she thought it was unreasonable, she intuitively felt that she should go ahead and pay the money to get the massage. The number is significant.

There are typically three characters driving the action in virtually all dramas. These three characters are the persecutor, the rescuer, and the victim. The dynamic among these three elements almost always ensures that things are going to change. Six is two times three, which in this case meant there were at least two things she needed to change.

There are 360 degrees in a circle. A circle is a symbol of the soul because it has no beginning and no end. Zero, the final number of the three, is a circle. The dream is saying that she needed to make at least two major (soul) changes and that she could do this within ten minutes (the amount of time for the proposed massage).

Several weeks after this symbolic interpretation, she discovered where the 360 number came from in a practical sense. She had put all of her household belongings into a storage locker prior to moving in with her daughter's family. She was feeling that she needed to move elsewhere. Living with her daughter helped with her finances, but she spent much of her time babysitting the two young girls. She enjoyed watching them occasionally, but felt that she was called upon too often to watch the girls. Her first decision was whether she would live alone or with others. There was the independence of living alone, which she missed; however, she was also feeling the need for companionship. She felt she also needed to reduce her rent. She concluded that she needed to live with a friend or lover.

Her second decision was whether she should live with one of several friends or with a lover. She had multiple possibilities. In a moment of clarity, she was able to make the above decisions within ten minutes if she listened to her gut. The decisions she made would cost her more than living with her daughter, but would give her adult company and independence. The symbolic interpretations emphasized that she needed to make at least two soulful decisions rapidly, which would cost her financially, while the practical discovery of the 360 storage locker number indicated what the content of those decisions would be (under what circumstances she would choose to live).

Jungian therapists or Jungians very much believe in the essential correctness of embodied emotion, which is sometimes experienced as a feeling in the gut or an intuitive relaxation response, because everything is going to be all right. This embodied emotion is right at least ninety percent of the time, assuming that the person is basically in sound mental health. A person who is seriously mentally imbalanced, such as a person with bipolar disorder who is experiencing a manic state, will make faulty decisions that are overly optimistic and vastly overestimate what actually can be accomplished.

With the above caveat, a person ignores their own inner voice at their own peril. It is the part of the mind that composes the majority of the psyche. It is the voice of the soul, the higher self, and/or the subconscious. They are all

pretty much the same thing. I have never met a client who wished that they hadn't listened to an inner voice.

Dream 32C: 25 or 624

A 36-year-old rock singer dreamt that he was in a liquor store. In the liquor store was a male movie star he disliked because of his arrogance and bravado. Half of the store was filled with toys. He went to the elevator, accompanied by a female cousin his same age who was very emotionally stable. He got on the elevator alone and sat on the floor of the elevator. The elevator did not move.

The dream shifted to his bedroom, where he was asleep with his wife. He awoke to find five people near his age or younger who were playing poker at the foot of their bed. He remembered that the time on the clock was exactly 5:26.

Dream 32C—Interpretation

He was recently concerned about the effect of drinking alcohol (the liquor store) upon his band's playing (the toys) music. The band was led by an arrogant man that he disliked. Going into an elevator symbolizes changing levels of consciousness. He leaves his feeling of emotional stability behind (his stable female cousin) to decide which way he should go. It is implied that his not knowing whether he was going to stay with his band puts him down (he sits on the bottom of the elevator) and leads to no change of consciousness, i.e., staying with the band is neither a move up or a move down—it is simply a static decision.

The current band he was in had six members. He was thinking of joining a band that had five members. He woke up (became conscious) realizing that joining the new band would be a gamble that he might take. The time is five to (two) six. He was debating whether to join a band with five members or stay in his current band of six. This dream illustrates how idiosyncratic the meanings can be of specific numbers or times in dreams. It is virtually certain that a non-rounded number that stands out in the dreamer's memory has a specific and important meaning for the dreamer.

CHAPTER 33:
ANIMALS

Key 33: Animals represent the source of our basic, instinctive animal energy. There is a rough correspondence between the size and/or power of the animal and the amount and intensity of the instinctive energy the animal represents.

Animals are frequent participants in dreams because

they represent the instinctive energy in the psyche. The many different types of animals allow dreams to give a quite nuanced and full view of energies involved in the dream to which the subconscious is calling attention. We have already dealt with domesticated cats and dogs and their representations of female and male affection.

Animals are frequent inhabitants of dreams. It behooves the dream interpreter to be familiar with the meanings the average dreamer's subconscious assigns to the different animals. The different animals each give a nuanced description of the dreamer's instinctive energy that is currently affecting her life. The energies below are the most frequent drives I have observed to be represented by different dream animals.

▫ Whales are frequent denizens of dreams because they are huge mammals that reside in the ocean (the unconscious). As such, they frequently represent huge reservoirs of energy located deep within the subconscious (whales are capable of swimming deep within the ocean.)

▫ Fish in a body of water indicates there is a reserve of psychic energy within the dreamer that can be used to improve functioning. The larger and more virulent the sea life, the more psychic resources the dreamer is viewed as having by the subconscious.

▫ A rat almost always has a negative connotation. They represent the energy in such nefarious activities such as the energy involved in betrayal ("ratting out" someone). Freud specifically thought that images of rats frequently were related

to sexual abuse, and this is true a surprising number of times. The thought in this case is comparing the sexual perpetrator as having the energy of a rat.

▫ Birds frequently represent a very free energy or freedom, as flight in dreams is almost spiritual. Specific types of birds infer different types of energy. Talking birds such as parrots bespeak of a far different energy than turkeys, for example.

▫ Cows relate to productive and passively conformist energy, as cows are peaceful animals that are dutifully herded for man's benefit. Similarly, sheep evoke images of following or of being timid. Counting sheep may be a subconscious effort to connect with passive conforming energy that dispels conscious worries.

▫ Horses frequently relate to power (we even speak of horse-power). Horses are also frequently connected to common sense. Waxing Freudian for a second, horses seem to frequently represent female sexual power.

▫ Buffalo are almost prehistoric herd animals that were nearly driven to extinction. Buffalo frequently represent old energy that was thought to be extinguished but is being used by the dream to suggest that some powerful energy from the past is still vital.

◽ Lions, tigers, and bears (oh my!) represent raw, untamed natural power. That probably explains why sports teams are frequently named after these animals. Predatory animals are embedded deep in the collective unconscious, as our ancestors fought and escaped from predators for millions of years. Wolves typically relate to being attacked by a pack of the energy of one's peers.

◽ Insects and ants frequently warn of infestation, which is sometimes the insidious invasion of the body by disease. The compulsive and detailed automaton organization of ants finds many metaphors in modern life. Spiders weave webs that may illustrate the situation that we created for ourselves (what a tangled web we weave when first we practice to deceive). Noxious beings such as scorpions or killer bees relate to fear of being attacked unpredictably and suddenly, without sufficient cause.

◽ Elephants typically indicate massive conscious energy that the dreamer can use in his life. Elephants are the largest and most powerful land animals. Similar to a whale denoting a huge amount of subconscious energy, elephants typically signal tremendous

conscious psychological resources within the dreamer. Elephants are also known for having good memories.

DREAM 33A: DON'T KILL THE ENERGY—SWIM WITH IT

A 35-year-old man dreamt that he and his business associates were catching fish from a dock on the ocean. They caught several very large rainbow fish. An overriding voice commanded him to "throw the fish back into the ocean." When he tried to throw the fish back into the ocean, the fish would not leave his hand. Instead, the momentum of the throw resulted in his catapulting himself into the ocean. His business associates, similarly, accidentally threw themselves into the ocean with the momentum generated from trying to throw large rainbow fish back into the ocean that would not leave their hands.

Underwater in the ocean, the men were totally comfortable and had gills that allowed them to breathe. Large blue whales quietly escorted them. They had harpoons and could have shot the whales, but the whole scene spoke to them that would be an unnecessary disturbance with likely lethal consequences. The whales showed them the way to a bright golden city at the bottom of the sea, where they were welcomed by the inhabitants. The native people, who also had gills, saw him and his business partners as being future suppliers of desired goods.

DREAM 33A—INTERPRETATION

The dream was giving advice about how he should handle his business emotionally. The ocean is the primordial symbol of the subconscious and emotions. Aquatic creatures indicate emotional energy because they inhabit water and are almost always good news. The fact that huge creatures, whales, accompanied the dreamer underwater indicated strong emotional energy.

The fish the men caught were rainbow colored, indicating that all the emotions were involved. Color emphasizes emotion, with the different colors standing for different emotions. He and his associates were starting an Internet business and wanted to do it alone, without help from other large commercial websites. They wanted to play it safe, which the dream would not allow them to do. They wanted to stay safely on the dock and remain separated from the environment they were trying to get energy (money) from. The dream demanded that they immerse themselves in the environment they were working in instead of trying to remain separate and "above it all."

The dream reassured them that they could survive in the larger Internet world and that they could coexist with the larger energies there. They were advised to peacefully coexist with the larger powers in order to get where they wanted to go. The dream instructed them that they could use the larger websites (and their whale load of influence) to lead them to customers that desired their goods. The dream provided support that their instinctive subconscious energy (the whales) would take them where they needed to go.

Dream 33B: A Rat Tell-Tail Tale

A 38-year-old man dreamt that he had a rat's tail growing on the upper gum of his teeth, enough so that he could feel a bump on his stiff upper lip. Each time he paid attention to the rat's tail, it grew longer, just as Pinocchio's nose grew each time Pinocchio told a lie. He was going to a banquet in a hotel filled with businessmen. The head waiter was an intimidating dark, strong man. He had a helpful assistant, who waited on the dreamer. People left the banquet hall one by one. The dreamer feared that they were somehow being hurt, but he never saw any evidence that they were being mistreated. He subsequently discovered that he was tied to his chair, with his hands behind his back in handcuffs.

Dream 33B—Interpretation

This was a corporate executive who regularly consulted with me regarding his dreams so that he could get insight into his subconscious view of the political dynamics within himself and his company. He recently was in the process of leaving a company to form a new company with friends, which did similar work. He was going to a party in the near future where he would meet with some of his previous coworkers from his old company. The dream was telling him emphatically not to "rat out" his new company by telling his old colleagues too much. The dream was saying that he should not lie or "tell tales" (tell tails) or he would experience negative consequences. He felt uneasy about how some of his coworkers, who transferred to the new company, were treated, but the dream indicated that no harm came to them, which was the bottom line. In any case, the dream was screaming that his hands were tied and there was not much he could do about it. He decided to keep quiet, and he and his colleagues successfully joined and formed the new company.

DREAM 33C: ABUSING YOUR INNER CASH COW

A 38-year-old man dreamt that he was viewing a farmer forcibly leading a cow roped to a tractor. The cow was resisting and was forced to move from the tugging pulls of the tractor. The farmer finally staked the cow in the middle of a barren corral with a minimum of rope. The dreamer then saw himself leap into the scene, demanding that the farmer release the cow. The farmer appeared bored and looked away. The dreamer sprang towards the farmer and cut his ear, saying, "If you do not listen to me, I'll cut it off next time."

DREAM 33C—INTERPRETATION

The farmer was the part of him that made a living off husbanding plant and animal resources (living off his growth and instincts). Animals represent instincts or predilections. The cow was the part of himself that he lived off, much like a farmer derives income from livestock. As such, the cow was his inner cash cow, which was being forced to do things that he did not want to do. He had little leeway (the short rope) and little nourishment/support on the job (the barren corral). His executive self was angry at his forcing himself through an unrewarding work situation. The dream warned the executive part of his psyche which lived off his labors that he had better listen to his instinctive needs.

At the second, or interpersonal, level of interpretation, he had a boss who did not listen to him and just expected him to keep the money coming in while listening to almost nothing the dreamer said.

Dream 33D: From the Horse's Mouth

A 48-year-old woman dreamt she saw a man in the distance approaching her. As he drew closer, she noticed that his mouth was like a horse's mouth. When the man reached her, he began talking about how he was an artist and a writer. He explained to her the multitude of projects he was completing.

The dream then shifted to her maternal grandparents' home in South Carolina. She was enjoying being there, but felt somewhat worried. She then saw herself as a teenager sleeping outside the house at night.

Dream 33D—Interpretation

The woman was a sober alcoholic, who wrote in her leisure time. In the first part of the dream, her subconscious gave her direct advice. She "heard it from the horse's mouth" that she should do something creative, i.e., write. The second part of the dream explained why her subconscious was recommending this remedy.

She enjoyed visiting her maternal grandparents, but her grandfather was an episodic alcoholic and he worried her. The grandfather in the dream represented the alcoholic part of her subconscious. Sleeping outside in a dream emphasized the subconscious feeling of vulnerability. Our ancestors quickly learned that it was much safer to sleep in a covered dwelling, preferably with a large group of people. Nighttime and sleeping within a dream tend to represent subconscious issues, while daytime usually represents conscious issues of which the person is aware. Overall, putting the two parts of the dream together, her subconscious was recommending that she engage in creative pursuits, i.e., writing, to decrease her subconscious anxiety that she might have cravings to drink.

DREAM 33E: SO TOTALLY WOLF-LIKE

A 14-year-old female teenager dreamt that her young, teenage best friends turned into werewolves and attacked her.

DREAM 33E—INTERPRETATION

This teenager was a very trusting friend who believed innocently and naively that her friends always told her the truth. The dream was a condensation interpersonally and intrapsychically. Intrapsychically, the female werewolves represented her own

immature emotional impulses. The dream was warning her that she was very prone to attack herself. Interpersonally, the dream meant that she should be less naive about her friends' motivations.

Dream 33F: Beware the Scorpion

A 25-year-old man dreamt that there was a scorpion near his swimming pool. He sprayed it with water. It became bigger as he sprayed water on it and backed it up until it fell into his swimming pool. He fished it out with a net. The scorpion was twice the size it was originally and was now pregnant and soon to give birth to a multitude of scorpions. He ran with the net and threw the scorpion into the campfire, which had already been built and was burning. He felt relieved.

Dream 33F—Interpretation

Animals represent our instincts. Here the emphasis was put on the aggressive instinct because scorpions are aggressive animals that strike without warning. Water is emotion. The dream was stating that when he became emotional, his aggressive instinct grew and fed on itself, resulting in a multitude of disturbed relationships.

He most recently was having trouble with his roommate and his sweetheart because he tended to react suddenly with overly aggressive remarks. He had bipolar disorder and was thinking of going off his medication. The message of the dream advised against discontinuing medication that helped him avoid being too irritable. The emotions in his sphere of influence (his swimming pool) needed to change, which is emphasized by the pregnant scorpion being thrown into the campfire.

Dream 33G: Suck It Up

A 44-year-old man dreamt that he was in a car with his father. His father was driving. The dreamer was about twelve, which was the age he was when his father died in an auto accident. They were riding along the top of a mountain range. In the distance they saw a huge reservoir of water. Suddenly, the dam burst open after a car crashed into it. A herd of buffalo in the valley struggled in the flood waters. The dreamer saw himself in the dream take a tube and suck on it so that he magically made most of the water disappear. About half of the herd of buffalo were able to survive the flood, thanks to his actions.

Dream 33G—Interpretation

This dream was a "big" dream that gave a visual demonstration of his life course. A huge amount of emotional energy (the water) went out of his emotional reservoir when his father died in a car accident. This loss of his father and the loss of emotional energy threatened his instinctive energy (the buffalo), so that he was in distress for a long time. The dream tried to reassure him by pointing out that part of the herd, which represented his instinctive energy, would survive the tragic loss of his father. He was able to eventually sort out his emotions so that he could effectively use his energy to accomplish goals.

The dream reassured him that he could save his energy by "sucking it up." The dream implied that he need not castigate himself for not conserving or saving his energy earlier. There was still enough of the buffalo herd (his instinctive energy) so that he could rebuild his life.

CHAPTER 34:
DREAM INCUBATION

Key 34: Asking your subconscious a question before going to sleep will produce an answer in subconscious form anywhere from fifty to eighty percent of the time, depending upon the quality of the incubation process and the consistency with which the incubation process is pursued.

The educational television program Nova (PBS, Public Broadcasting System, Nova, What Are Dreams? August 2012) provided an excellent summary of dream research. In this summary, researchers found that by asking a question before going to sleep, the dreamer would produce a dream answer to the question around fifty percent of the time. Often the answer is in such cryptic form that it may not be recognized as dealing with the question. If the subconscious did a good job of disguising the answer into a form that we may accept, the dream is usually not understandable at a conscious level. An experienced dream interpreter, with the guidance of a coherent theory such as Jungian dream interpretation, will frequently recognize that a dream does indeed relate to the question, if not answer the question completely.

The process of getting the subconscious ready to answer a question is called dream incubation (Bernard, 2009). There are steps to the dream incubation process which, in this author's experience, proceed best in the following sequence:

▫ Prior to going to sleep, the dreamer formulates the question. The question should preferably be in the dreamer's own words. The law of parsimony is operative here, as the more direct and clear the question, the more likely that the dream produced will give a substantial answer.

◻ Once the question is formulated, the dreamer needs to write the question out in his own writing at least three times. The purpose of this step is not to keep a record of the question as much as it is intended to register the question deep within the dreamer's subconscious. There is something very subconscious about writing—we do it without thinking.

◻ The most important step is that the dreamer writes down the dream as soon as she/he awakens. It does not matter if the dreamer dreamt of Daffy Duck—the experienced interpreter needs to hear the dream in as much detail as possible. Again, the images often will not make conscious sense, but are frequently discernible as a direct answer to the question by an experienced dream interpreter.

DREAM 34A: SAVE THE KITTY

A 43-year-old woman dreamt she went into a public ethnic marketplace that was empty. She could hear the squealing cries of a mother cat for her kittens. She somehow found a bowl, which she filled with milk. She never saw the mother cat. After she scrubbed the bowl, a beautiful kitten emerged from the liquid milk. As she reached to remove the kitten from the milk, a green serpent, with a face like hers, ominously crouched in the milk, getting ready to strike.

DREAM 34A—INTERPRETATION

She had to pass a test in order to leave her current job for more financially rewarding employment. She, inexplicably, had failed the test twice. This dream was the result of her incubating a dream by writing the question, "Why am I having trouble passing the test?" three times before going to sleep. There is something very subconscious about writing, as we do it quickly and without much forethought. The purpose of writing it down is not to keep a record of the question, but to ingrain the question in the dreamer's subconscious, so that it is more likely that the dreamer will have a dream addressing the issue.

In the dream, the commercial public marketplace indicated that the dream was about her work life. The mother cat that she never saw represented her thought that she should give birth to a new aspect of her instincts. Kittens represent affectionate feelings and frequently refer to female affections (not necessarily so, but frequently so). She was having difficulty leaving her current job because of the many good friends there (affection).

The most important part is for the dreamer to write down whatever they remember upon awakening. Even if she dreams about Porky Pig, it is likely to be related to the incubation question. The subconscious uses its own logic; that became clearly discernible to me after attempting to interpret dreams for about twenty-five years. This book will help you lessen the time to your own inner dream interpreter epiphanies.

She liked her current workplace and felt nurtured within it. Cleaning the bowl and putting milk in it was her preparing herself for a new workplace. The beautiful kitten was the dream trying to reassure her that she could find a new and fond place with nurturing and affectionate feelings.

Snakes represent change, as they are one of the few animals to completely shed their skin. Green is the color of growth. The dream was saying that she was afraid that if she reached out for a job change, that the change and growth might destroy the support/nurture she desired from work.

DREAM 34B: YOU ARE MUCH TOO WORRIED

A 56-year-old man incubated a dream regarding whether having penile implant surgery would be beneficial for him. He wrote three times on a sheet of paper, "Would having penile implant surgery be beneficial?" before he went to sleep to ingrain the question in his subconscious. He dreamt that night that he was climbing along a ledge on a cliff that inclined gradually upward. The ledge was three feet wide, and he could easily and safely have walked upright. He crawled instead of walking and made very slow progress. He felt terrified, even though there were no breaks or irregularities to the path.

DREAM 34B—INTERPRETATION

The dream was giving a positive answer to the question he asked. Although he would have to make some effort (climbing a cliff), his subconscious was telling him that he could do it safely. He was much too worried and fearful of the surgery. It is notable that the dream presented no insurmountable barriers and he neither fell nor came close to falling.

DREAM 34C: ARRRRGGH!

Before going to sleep, the dreamer wrote out the question, "How can I improve the relationship part of my life?" He repetitively wrote out the question three times in order to ingrain it in his subconscious. In the morning, he faithfully recorded the following dream.

The dreamer was a 38-year-old man. He dreamt that his older and physically abusive brother, with whom the dreamer disagreed on virtually everything, appeared as a pirate in the bar/mess hall of the pirate ship. The dreamer was seated near the back of the bar, while the abusive older brother was on a stage, making various bombastic statements. At one point, the abuser bellowed to a room filled with bloodcurdling pirates, "Ninety percent of relationships with women are bilge water."

DREAM 34C—INTERPRETATION

The dream answered his question directly. He was having trouble in his marriage because he discounted his wife and did not listen to her closely enough. The dream used the most graphic images it possibly could to make the point that his condescending and disregarding attitude toward his wife was intolerable and needed to change. The dreamer subsequently resolved, that when his wife talked to him when he was on the computer, he would force himself to walk to a different chair and listen to her while looking directly at her eyes. He thought it would come close to killing him if he forced himself to do this, but the results were palpable and nothing but positive. A little listening went a long way in improving his relationship with his wife. No wonder people have two ears and one mouth.

DREAM 34D: WHAT IDEAS WILL FLY?

A 48-year-old man was starting a business that sold school clothes for girls from ages eight to eleven years old. He decided to incubate a dream that asked, "How can I best manage my business?" He dreamt that he and his daughters were mixing batter for cookies. Eventually, the batter took to the air, traveling around the kitchen, with some of the batter sticking to the wall before coming back and landing in the bowl from which the batter originated. He saw himself then making two kinds of cookies. One kind used brown sugar to create very sweet cookies that had a Hershey's Kiss in the middle. The other batter was used to make chocolate chip cookies. There was no doubt in his mind that the Hershey kiss cookies were much better than the chocolate chip cookies.

DREAM 34D—INTERPRETATION

The dream was advising him to show his product around the world, to give it plenty of "air" time on the Internet, as it was a web based business. His young daughters could help him determine which ideas were likely "to stick to the wall." Through the cookies, the dream was advising what his approach to his business should be to get the best results. According to the dream, he should use a "sweet" approach (the brown sugar cookies) that emphasized emotion and love (the Hershey kiss). The dream is indicating that using mostly original material (the brown sugar batter was original) that he mixed up with some prefabricated commercial material (the Hershey Kiss) would be preferable to simply reselling manufactured goods (like the prefabricated chocolate chips in the other cookies). Dreams can sometimes help guide business plans.

CHAPTER 35:
QUESTIONS

Key 35: Dreams can best be regarded as metaphors that relate directly to the dreamer's issues.

As such, the interpreter needs to gather information by asking about the dreamer's circumstances and issues in life. The issues can range from metaphysical to concrete physical health issues. Questions can be formed most efficaciously, in my humble opinion, by using Dr. Carl Jung's dream interpretation, supplemented with the keys from this book.

Questions can be formulated from a theoretical basis by using the keys outlined here. It many times leads to questions that may not be asked otherwise. For example, someone dreaming of an apocalypse could be asked, "Does it seem like part of your world is coming to an end?" Knowing that each character is a part of the dreamer's psyche and that males go with actions and females go with emotions helps to formulate questions. Identification of an archetype in a dream, and there are many more archetypes than those described here, opens up very rich sources of inquiry.

When a dreamer indicates that a character in the dream is like someone in real life, you want to ask (1) about how old was the dreamer when they knew that person, and (2) what was that person's personality like? When the dreamer gives the description of the personality and when that personality was in their life, they are basically telling what part of the psyche is appearing in the dream. It is much the same with animals that appear in dreams, although animals tend to be more instinctive and more predictable, according to what species they are. If a dreamer talks about a family pet, one wants to ask what the pet was like and how the dreamer felt about the pet. Descriptions of animals are giving information about what instincts are involved in the dream and how those instincts are manifesting in the dreamer's life in particular situations. As the dreamer describes, preferentially in detail, what characters and animals are present in a dream, they are telling you which important parts of the psyche are involved in the dream.

Ghosts, aliens and monsters are indications of spiritual, foreign and/or parts of themselves that are mysterious, unknown or unacceptable to the dreamer. If a character is unlike one the dreamer knew in real life, have the dreamer describe the figure in as much detail as possible. The figure may represent a familiar archetype or simply be a part of the dreamer himself that the dreamer does not recognize. It is frequently the case that the dreamer does not recognize a character. That is because the character may be a new part of the psyche. The subconscious decided that the dreamer was ready for and now could handle becoming gradually aware of a previously unknown part of themselves. Many unknown parts reside in the **Shadow** that are not negative but are simply unknown. The dreamer is more likely to be more adaptive in life if the dreamer has access to a greater variety of parts in their psyche to use.

Knowledge of the archetypes and how different gendered characters tend to act reveals processes going on within the dreamer. It is explication of these processes that is most helpful to clients. There is no way that the dream interpreter knows enough of the details of a person's life to supply the entire interpretation. In this paradigm, the dream interpreter becomes more the identifier of possible processes and archetypes residing within the dreamer. The client becomes the supplier of vital biographical and emotional information. The interpreter supplies the framework and the dreamer supplies the specific content that relates to that framework.

Dream 35A: You Can Go Your Own Way

A 24-year-old man dreamt that he was watching an airplane coming in for a crash landing. He saw himself from a distance getting out of the airplane, standing on the wing, and jumping safely to the beach of an island. The plane continued on and crashed some distance away in the ocean.

Dream 35A—Interpretation

My first question to this client was, "Have you been pursuing a goal with your highest ideals, but feel now that you have to abandon it?" He said that was exactly what was occurring in his life. He had started a creative writing club and had high aspirations for it. There were only four people in the club, and he was its vice president. The president of the club was a woman with whom he disagreed on nearly every major issue that came up. She wanted to limit the club to just the four members, while he envisioned an active community with scores of members. There was no compromising, as she would not accept anything less than exactly what she wanted.

The question was based on the metaphor the dream presented to him. Flight is usually almost spiritual in dreams and usually involves high ideals. The dream was assuring him that he could abandon an endeavor that was bound to crash (in this case because of differences with the president). It assured him he could land safely from such a departure, although he would feel extremely anxious doing it. One of his major issues in therapy was having extreme difficulty telling others what he really thought. On the basis of this dream, he assertively left the club and gave them ample reasons why he was leaving, so that it would not be misinterpreted. It was a growth experience for him, as he never envisioned himself being able to stand up for his goals.

DREAM 35B: THREATENING BIRDBRAINS

A 48-year-old man dreamt that he was outside and three parakeets were flying toward him. Each parakeet carried a rattlesnake tail that made the threatening rattlesnake noise. The birds were each half alive and half stuffed animal.

DREAM 35B—INTERPRETATION

He recently had received a letter from a consumer agency regarding a complaint made by a customer. He thought that the claim was frivolous and had no basis. He, nevertheless, was worried about the implications of having the consumer agency involved in the complaint.

The dream was making several comments. To elicit information, I asked the question, as would Jungian dream analyst, Jeremy Taylor, or popular dream interpreter, Joyce Delaney, if there was a situation where he felt threatened. He explained the above situation, which the dream commented upon extensively with the image it presented.

He first thought was that the people complaining were "birdbrains" engaging in a "lot of loose talk" (parakeets who learn to talk do so in a repetitive and mechanical manner). The rattlesnake tails with their threatening noise indicated his fears about the consumer agency involvement. It was significant that only the snakes' tails and not their venomous heads were involved. The dream was saying that there was a lot of threatening noise, which had no bite to it. There was also the suggestion that the dream might think he needed to change without specifying what things needed to be changed.

There were prominent indicators of change in the dream. A snake is a symbol of change, since it is one of a few animals that completely sheds its skin. The number three is the number of change, as having three people in a relationship guarantees that there will be unstable change. The three birds being half alive and half stuffed animal was a comment by the dream to the effect of "are these people for real?"

Dream 35C: Getting My Goat

The following dream is being presented because it contains a question the dreamer long entertained regarding his family.

A 48-year-old professional race car driver dreamt that he and a jury were at his house. Strangely, he felt that they were all waiting for a verdict to be announced as to whether he and the jury were guilty or not guilty. He then went to his garage and looked at an expensive table saw he used to make furniture for his family. He also looked at the office, where he did freelance work on his computer. He then looked outside to see a dog nursing a goat. He then went to the bathroom and took a shower.

Dream 35C—Interpretation

The dream screamed that he was being judged for being judgmental, which was exactly how he felt in his family. His going to the garage was representative of the things he did to cope with pressure he felt from his family. One activity was to constructively divert himself while being supportive of the family (making furniture). The other was to support the family by bringing in extra income by working through the computer. The strange image of a dog nursing a goat had multiple meanings. The goat represented the part of him that felt like a scapegoat. Dogs are usually masculine affection. The dream was saying that he was being made to feel like a scapegoat when he desperately wanted to be nurtured by his family, toward whom he felt affectionate and supportive.

Going to the bathroom to "clean up" usually means that the dreamer needs to change whatever immediately preceded it in the dream. The dream was saying that it was strange for him to expect to be nurtured as long as he accepted the role of being a scapegoat for the family. His reaction to the family was frequently "Are you kidding me?" It is notable that a "kid" is a young goat. It was also the case that after a family member said something especially derogatory toward the dreamer, they minimized the meaning of the statement by insisting that they were just "kidding." He needed to revise the image being offered to him by his family because it was really "getting his goat."

CHAPTER 36:
LUCID DREAMS

Key 36: Lucid dreams are of limited value.

Many people view lucid dreams as the ultimate. They see it as permission from the mind to do anything their hearts desire; however, lucid dreams are of limited or no value to the dream interpreter. When trying to untangle a lucid dream, it becomes apparent that the conscious portion of the psyche invaded the subconscious dream world. Whatever insights might have been obtained from interpretations of the subconscious dream world are spoiled by the dreamer's conscious desires. Lucid dreams often appear to be more the expression of the desire to have magical powers. They use the subconscious for conscious wish fulfillment and are unlikely to give the dreamer new direction or insight because lucid dreams for the most part ignore the subconscious elements of the dream. The dream in the hands of the conscious simply becomes a playground to do things that cannot be accomplished in reality.

DREAM 36A: I BELIEVE I CAN FLY

A 21-year-old college student dreamt that a nuclear explosion went off five miles from his house. He was somehow unhurt, but wondered if he would get cancer from the radiation because he smoked. He was transported to looking into the doorway to a bar, and the door was slammed in his face. He then saw his father driving a car in which the dreamer was a passenger, which was headed to Mexico. Members of two major drug cartels were shooting at them from each side of the road. His father was hit in the throat and bled bright red blood, but was still able to keep driving. They then came upon Mideast terrorist extremists, who stopped them and questioned his father's religious beliefs in loud voices.

At the very end, the dream turned into a lucid dream where he was trying to fly, but he could not get off the ground. He finally found himself stranded, floating aimlessly in outer space.

DREAM 36A—INTERPRETATION

This dream was screaming to him about his recently increased substance abuse. The dream exaggerated ridiculously to get his attention, i.e., he had better quit smoking or he could die from cancer (nuclear bomb exaggeration). The dream punctuated the advice that he should quit drinking by slamming a saloon door in his face. Literally, illegal drugs were affecting his father introject, the major part of the personality used to get things done.

The drug cartels represented the **Shadow** addicted parts of himself. The drugs injured him (the drug cartels shooting) by taking away his life force (blood) and reducing his creativity (his father is wounded in the throat chakra which, according to the traditions of India, is the chakra most associated with creativity). His father was a blustery man who held rigidly to fundamentalist and stern religious beliefs (the dreamer felt conflicted with his father introject which is why there is questioning of religious beliefs in the dream). The dream was warning him to quit smoking, reduce his drinking and stop abusing dangerous drugs, as these threatened his life, creativity, and ability to get things done.

At the end of the dream, his subconscious would not let him fly, which he very much enjoyed, because it was punishing him for abusing substances too much. In this dream, the attempt to become fully lucid is defeated by the subconscious as a warning to the dreamer to stop abusing substances. The **Shadow** (the drug cartels) earlier used violence against the dreamer to grab his attention, i.e., to get him to stop using drugs now. A nuclear explosion is instant change which the dream was dramatically demanding from him.

CHAPTER 37:
LIKE FROM ANOTHER
PLANET, MAN

Key 37: When interpreting a symbol, it often is best to interpret the symbol as if the interpreter were from another planet.

An interpreter wants to focus on the most basic and central meaning of the symbol. Such a point of view would not work in everyday conversation, where we assume that almost everyone in a given culture is conversant with the common meaning of everyday words. It is the common meaning of a word, term, idiom or saying that the dream is most often using in a concrete way to convey a meaning to the dreamer. We typically do not question whether other people in our culture, unless they are mentally challenged, understand the basic meanings of words we have been familiar with since we were seven years old or younger. It is a way of thinking that takes some getting used to, for the interpreter assumes that the dream did not include items that had no meaning. As can be seen, many of the interpretations of specific items are not particularly psychological and rely on rational deduction taken to such an extreme that people in real life would be taken aback.

DREAM IMAGE 37A: YOU'RE IN THE ARMY NOW

A 42-year-old engineer dreamt that he was walking through the woods when he came to a clearing. In the clearing there was an armed personnel carrier.

DREAM IMAGE 37A—INTERPRETATION

What is an armed personnel carrier? It is a Defense Department equipment vehicle used to move people employed by the government. What is a clearing? It is where things become clear. With data provided by the dreamer, interpretation of the dream is elementary, my dear Watson.

The company that the engineer worked for recently received a defense contract from the government that required him to receive a security clearance ("a clearing") that would require him to move to a new area of the company (which is the reason why there was an army "personnel carrier"—because he would be moved inside the company because of the new government defense contract).

It is often helpful to consider what sayings could be derived from the image. One that occurs is "he's not out of the woods yet." Things would not be settled and clear until he received a security clearance.

DREAM IMAGE 37B: SOME KIND OF A DILDO?

A 26-year-old man dreamt that he was looking through his mother's chest of drawers. All the drawers were full of dildos.

DREAM IMAGE 37B—INTERPRETATION

This dream pinpointed that he was having panic attacks due primarily to his mother introject, which is mainly related to emotional issues. The dream pointed out that his mother introject was literally screwing him up. Part of the reason his panic attacks were so disabling was that the more he had panic attacks, the more he obsessed and worried about having panic attacks which, of course, virtually guaranteed that he would have more panic attacks. He needed therapy to help break the cycle of anxiety. His panic attacks literally amounted to "mental masturbation."

Chapter 38:
The Devil Is in
the Details

Key 38: Every dream detail has meaning.

Symbols used in a dream are often combinations of multiple symbols with multiple meanings. The end result is an unusual or fantastic symbol. The resulting condensation is the minimum number of symbols the unconscious is using to convey meaning in the dream. The dream seeks to provide the most information it can in the smallest possible psyche space. The unconscious condenses the symbols into the most potent and attention-grabbing symbols the dream possibly can derive. Years of interpreting dreams leaves one with sober respect for the often significant impact of seemingly trivial details. There are no trivial details in a dream. Each detail is in the dream with the consent of the subconscious, which believes that the detail provided is just the right symbol to convey understanding to the dreamer that is the most helpful.

Dream 38A: That Rumor Has Legs

A 28-year-old senior in college dreamt that he belonged to a fraternity. They owned a magic box. The fraternity members would tear up pieces of paper into little bits and then put the pieces into the box. All members of the fraternity contributed their share of torn-up paper to the magic box. Then they would shake the contents of the box up before dumping it out on a lawn. The pieces of paper coming from the box would form a shocking message on the lawn. Eventually a stick figure man would come to life from the pieced- together message.

DREAM 38A—INTERPRETATION

The fraternity was in great conflict over rumors and misinformation created by some members against other members. The dream was saying that their brotherhood, the fraternity, was prone to piece together little pieces of information into shocking misinformation, which eventually came to live a life of its own. His subconscious was warning the dreamer about his participation in creating havoc in other people's lives by giving rumors life magically, because they would not exist without the fraternity's efforts.

The havoc created by the divisive groups within the fraternity was mirrored in his own conflicted psyche. He felt dishonest and traitorous about giving life to unwarranted stories that were largely made up. He was creating divisiveness between parts of his mind. His own psyche was betraying him because he was not living up to standards he set for himself. Ironically, he was participating in this pernicious process out of misplaced loyalty to troublemakers within the fraternity.

DREAM 38B: JUST SHIP IT

A 28-year-old man dreamt that he was working at a UPS mail store. In the front office were two colleagues. One was a beautiful woman. The other was a somewhat older, quirky man who was unpredictably abrasive with customers. In the back office were a very professional older woman and an executive who was super confident and likable. A customer came in with a snow globe of the sort that is filled with water. The figures inside depict a winter scene and, when you shake the crystal bowl, it looks like it is snowing. The customer noted that he wanted it shipped far away and was willing to pay for it to be handled with extra care.

Dream 38B—Interpretation

He was working in a retail store. He was well thought of by other employees, but every so often a difficult customer would rub him the wrong way and he would tell the customer off. The back office represented his underlying potential at work. He was capable of very positive emotions (the beautiful **Anima** woman) and competent action (the cool **Zeus Archetype** executive). The dream assured him that he was capable of positive emotional interaction with virtually all customers (the beautiful woman in the front office) while noting that there was a quirky part of himself prone to act rashly.

The snow globe represented encapsulated negative emotions. This item is critical in the interpretation of this dream and needs to be dissected. Water is subconscious emotion. A cold winter scene surrounded by water in a globe is encapsulated cold emotions. The dream left no doubt as to how he should treat customers. He should handle customers with care and distance himself from cold emotions. In regard to his sometimes brass actions with difficult customers, he should simply "ship it."

CHAPTER 39:
DIFFERENT KINDS
OF DREAMS

Key 39: There are at least five different categories of dreams: predictive dreams, post traumatic stress dreams, symbolic dreams, dreams of desire, and vision dreams. Identifying what type of dream is being presented helps interpretation considerably. Each type calls for a certain response from the interpreter and the dreamer.

1. The Predictive Dream

One type of dream is the predictive dream. A sign that the dream is predictive is that it remains static and unchangeable, regardless of how the dreamer chooses to work on it. The predictive dream is frequently a warning about events that have not yet occurred.

If a dream was puzzling and had a cryptic character whose intentions were not clear, Dr. Carl Jung would sometimes use a procedure he called active imagination. In this procedure, the dreamer typically relaxes when awake and tries to re-dream the dream in as much detail as they can until they reach the point where they want to ask the puzzling character a question. Frequently, the effect is like writing a fictional book in the sense that at some point the book almost writes itself, because there are only so many ways the writer can go after constructing a given situation with complex characters. The character gives useful answers if the dreamer can give full rein to his or her conscious imagination. It is exceedingly difficult to give conscious imagination the breadth of freedom it needs to approach subconscious insight.

Active imagination was used by this therapist earlier in my work, but this procedure mostly does not deliver the information being sought. The problem with the procedure is that one is using mostly conscious processes. Similar to the problem of trying to interpret lucid dreams, the answer given may be more conscious wish fulfillment than subconscious insight. One is likely to obtain the answer one wants to hear rather than the answer one needs to hear to improve functioning. The insight experience many times is not so much an "Aha!" experience as it is an "Oh no!" experience.

Using procedures like active imagination will not work with a predictive or clairvoyant dream. With a predictive dream, the characters do not answer the questions. No other possible different courses of action are considered or even generated. It just stays the same and seems immutable and impermeable.

Predictive dreams can be quite startling and give the interpreter questions about the nature of true reality. I once had a psychic woman who dreamt that a major airliner crashed in a ball of fire when taking off from Paris. Two weeks later, the supersonic Concorde crashed in a fireball upon takeoff from Paris.

A more pedestrian predictive dream is described below. This dream happened before the events that the dream warned about occurred. The philosophical questions are at least twofold. First, is there some kind of record of partially determined future reality in the collective unconscious that the dreamer's personal subconscious becomes tied into that is reflected in a predictive dream? Or, is the dreamer's subconscious, in its quest to help the dreamer solve problems, constructing the scenarios that are most likely to occur in the dreamer's life?

The law of parsimony leads me to favor the second possibility. Still, a person wonders about a partially determined universe. Carolyn Myss, medical intuitive and a leader of New Age thinking who is also well versed in Jungian dream interpretation, proposed that life is somewhat like a computer program. There are critical choice points that send life into determined directions, so that the other possibilities that were not chosen could not occur. In this scheme, it is our choices at critical stages of development that send us down a certain venue until another choice point is reached. Considering both questions and both possibilities, there is probably only one sensible answer. Yes.

DREAM 39A: THE TRIMMING AND SKIMMING OF THE RANCH

A 42-year-old lawyer who grew up on a ranch in Montana dreamt that his brother John, who was five years younger, was trimming the hooves of one of their prize racehorses while the dreamer watched from a short distance. His brother was trimming the horse's hooves in a very unusual way. The horse was essentially thrown down on a piece of large plywood across an old and worn out carpenter's bench in a clumsy and almost impossibly difficult setup. The horse was white and named Snowy. Suddenly his two older, physically abusive brothers, who looked like professional wrestlers, appeared and ran toward the dreamer. The animal was startled and jumped up in a commotion. His brother John moved to the side and was unhurt. His father was in the background and tried to warn the dreamer to get out of there as fast as he could. The dreamer was mesmerized by the situation and felt like he could not move. Snowy then staggered toward the dreamer. Snowy staggered like a drunken alcoholic and the dreamer actually worried that the horse might stumble and fall on him.

DREAM 39A—INTERPRETATION

As will be explained below, this dream occurred about six months before his parents' death in a car accident. The hardest thing to remember in dream interpretation is that at the first and intrapsychic level of interpretation, each character and animal in the dream represents a part of the dreamer's psyche. This lawyer, until his mid-twenties, had worked hard on his father's ranch in his youth and throughout college and law school. He subsequently went to live in New York, where he was a successful lawyer. His brother stayed on the ranch and rented the land out while pursuing additional businesses, such as bars and nightclubs, which came to consume almost all of his time.

His brother used the racehorses and the ranch as equity, which allowed him to buy alcohol related businesses. He also did investing for his retired parents, and they amassed a considerable portfolio of real estate. The parents were involved in a fatal car accident and there were no survivors.

It was discovered that his brother had all of his parent's property put into a trust which he alone inherited, in spite of his having five other siblings, who all worked on the ranch at different points in their lives. His brother, more or less, legally stole all of his siblings' inheritance. No one questioned that he should have received a larger portion of the estate, but it was ridiculous for him to legally steal a ranch on which the entire family had worked for at least sixty years. He did not offer even a token sharing of the inheritance. It was a slap in the face to all his siblings.

His brother was totally unleashed after his parents died. He made a series of increasingly risky investments and refused to walk away from any of the bad deals. He went through the entire inheritance in less than a year.

Looking at the dream psychologically, his brother represented the part of the dreamer that worked on the ranch. Trimming Snowy amounted to meaning that the dreamer's ego was trying to trim his instinctive support (the animal supports the ranch financially and hooves support the horse physically) for the ranch (the racehorse is the money producer for the ranch, and trimming the hooves was advice from the dream to the dreamer to cut back on his instinctive support of the ranch).

The dream was warning the dreamer that trying to help the ranch financially was misguided. His instinctive desire to help his family was not going to work. The lawyer dreamer had obsessively and needlessly worried about his parents' financial health, even paying for a hired hand to work there for fifteen months at one point. For this lawyer, the ranch was a mental trap that mesmerized him.

The lawyer had two older, physically abusive brothers, who were huge and menacing. Their sudden appearance in the dream startled the racehorse, which was saying that the **Shadow** abusers deeply scared the dreamer, to the point that his instincts became unsteady. The lawyer still had remnant anxiety from the abuse he suffered as a child.

The whole setup (the workbench and plywood) was almost impossibly arranged. No good was to come from it. The dreamer's instincts (Snowy) to help his family and the ranch were likely to be hurt (from his brother John "trimming," i.e., skimming, the ranch financially). The dreamer himself was likely to get hurt by the situation. That Snowy staggered like a drunken alcoholic was a warning that his instincts did not see the situation clearly and that the dreamer was instinctively addicted to the ranch.

It is notable that his father was a disabled man who was ignored by the abusers and terrorized by his wife. There was no love in the marriage. The children were raised like cattle, as a cash crop to work on the ranch and keep it going. Snow is frozen water, i.e., cold emotion. The racehorse being named Snowy is another case of the dream making even all the details close to perfect.

The father did have a relationship with the dreamer and was the one who finally called the police after the abusers went overboard in their abuse of the dreamer and inflicted considerable physical injury upon the dreamer. The abuse stopped after the intervention by the courts, which probably explained why he became a lawyer. His father had faults, but was an essentially decent man who saved the dreamer.

This dream occurred six months before the parents' deaths. The estate was impossibly arranged so that no good could come from it because his brother basically stole the ranch. The dreamer, with the help of therapy, was able to avoid being tricked into helping his brother further financially prior to the parents' deaths. Unbelievably, his brother and mother constantly bewailed their supposedly poor financial condition to the dreamer. His brother was a liar who self-righteously proclaimed that he and he alone was the only one deserving of an inheritance.

Indeed, no good came from the estate being put entirely in his brother's name. His brother declared bankruptcy less than two years after the parents died. True to form, after the bankruptcy, his brother continued to ask the dreamer and relatives for money to support his ventures.

2. THE POST TRAUMATIC STRESS DREAM

The post traumatic stress dream is the second type. DSM-4, the diagnostic manual for mental health, allows post traumatic stress disorder (PTSD) to be diagnosed on the basis of recurrent vivid nightmares of traumatic life-threatening events that actually occurred. There is no interpretation needed with PTSD dreams. In this case, the dream is a memory burned into the dreamer's subconscious. The memory stays as fresh with the dreamer as if it occurred yesterday. It is exactly what happened in the past. Combat, armed robberies, gang wars, serious traffic accidents and natural disasters, for example, are the content of PTSD dreams.

3. THE SYMBOLIC DREAM

The third type is the dream that is symbolic and can be interpreted in line with Sigmund Freud or Carl Jung. Freud, the originator of psychotherapy beginning in the early part of the twentieth century, mainly looked backward. Freud was trying to discover how the main traumatic events of the past were affecting the person's thoughts and behaviors now. On the other hand, Jung tried to assess the person's current projections and proclivities. The defenses and habitual ways of dealing with conflicts strongly influence the future. In any given dream, there were personal elements coming from the dreamer and/or archetypal elements coming from the dreamer's culture.

In any case, symbolic dreams could be subconscious predictions of what was likely to transpire if the dreamer stayed on his present course in life. By changing what the dreamer focused upon in the here and now, the dreamer could change the course of his or her life. The majority of the dreams in this book are symbolic dreams.

4. DREAMS OF DESIRE

This type of dream is the colloquial meaning of dreaming. To dream is to wish for something that you desire but do not have. Children less than five years old have dreams that are virtually always dreams of desire. Dreams of a defined goal, such as a house or car, are dreams of desire.

Lucid dreams are essentially dreams of desire. Lucid dreams occur when the dreamer suddenly realizes that he is dreaming and can do magical dreamlike activities like breathing under water or flying like Superman within the dream, at his leisure. Lucid dreams can be thought of as having consciousness within a dream. Lucid dreams are the ego intruding on the subconscious. This may be because the dreamer's ego does not want to hear the implied message from the dream. Lucid dreams represent ego consciousness taking over the dream process and using the subconscious as a magical playground. For example, who has not wanted to be able to fly like Superman/Superwoman at some point in his or her life?

5. Dream Visions

Dream visions are very special. They typically involve the dreamer having a dream of a deceased loved one that is so very vivid that it seems like the loved one was actually present with them. These dreams are often life changing. They typically are trying to reassure, warn or provide useful information to the dreamer. Dream visions often have a transforming effect upon the dreamer.

Dream Vision 39A: Go On and Live a Good Life

Years ago, when I was beginning my private practice as a psychologist, a 38-year-old man presented himself to me because he desired treatment for panic attacks that occurred at least once per day. The panic attacks started after a horrible event.

He, his wife, two young children, a sister he was close to, and his mother all got into a van to go to a family reunion. He forgot something at the house. They were running late. He told his wife that he would go into the house and retrieve the item and would drive a different family vehicle alone to the reunion. Part of the thinking was that it was possible that some members of the family might prefer to leave the family reunion earlier than the others. And then, tragedy struck.

An out-of-control semi-truck hit them head on at a high speed and they were all killed. He started to have panic attacks, I want to say understandably, on a daily basis. We tried all manner of cognitive, relaxation and behavioral therapy. Nothing worked. The tragedy was too much for his emotions to bear. I then decided to suggest that he keep track of his dreams, because knowing what was going on with him subconsciously might give us an idea of the best way to proceed with therapy.

A week later, he came back with good news.

"I no longer have panic attacks," he said. What in the world could have turned things around one hundred eighty degrees this fast, I mused. He went on to explain, "I will tell you that this was a dream, but I want you to understand that it did not feel like a dream to me. I was very emotionally close to my sister (who was only one year older than the dreamer). It felt like my sister appeared to me, as I was sleeping, to explain that the accident was instantaneous death. She said that none of them suffered beyond a millisecond, and that they had all moved on to a better place. She assured me that they would be available to me in spirit. Most of all, they all wanted me to continue to live the best life that I could."

He did not have one panic attack after having that vision dream. He asked me whether I thought he saw his sister or whether I thought it was a dream. I mostly avoided the question by saying that I did not care, the important thing was that the panic attacks were gone.

At moments like these, one is left wondering how much we really do know about the universe. It seems the more information astrophysicists gain about the universe, the more questions are generated. After interpreting dreams for years, I still find there are no limits as to how impressive dreams can be.

CHAPTER 40:
DREAM ON

Key 40: Big Dreams consistently give variations of advice that are related to the admonition, "To Thine Own Self Be True."

There is a reason all of the major religions converge upon the same truths. That is because people are human beings wherever they live in the world. Humans all have subconscious parts of their mind that are continuously evaluating how much psychological stress the person is able to take at any given time. It turns out that the above advice is the most adaptive for the individual and for the world.

Psychotherapy is mainly about finding what is true, I mean really true, for the client. Many mental health disturbances result from a physical or psychological assault on our integrity, whether that be physical integrity or self-esteem. Mental disorder is often a response to the constant assaults by the world upon the individual.

The true meanings of dreams are frequently disguised to protect the innocent and the guilty parts of the dreamer. The unconscious is protective and tries to evaluate how much insight the dreamer is prepared to hear. Dreams are constantly pushing the envelope of what the dreamer needs to know. Dreams are right next to the border of what one is ready to accept regarding one's life situation. Dreams are usually full of what the dreamer just now may be able to handle if it is delivered correctly in a dream.

Dreams are a way of getting around the dreamer's resistance to the full truth. The fact that the information is in the dream usually indicates that the dreamer may just now be able to accept the advice, warning or prescription from his subconscious. Dreams usually expose what is really going on.

Dreams will disguise the information to increase acceptance of the information by the dreamer.

Dreams are a way of helping the dreamer get past his resistance to hearing unpleasant truths. The dream often takes the dreamer's resistance by surprise. The dreamer has the experience, when given a correct interpretation, of facing needed and helpful truths. The subconscious is well aware that too much insight can be overwhelming to the dreamer.

When overwhelmed, the person's resistance to the truth is hardened and fortified by excessive rationalizations. An overly heavy insight could be more than the dreamer is ready to handle consciously. The subconscious doles out what conflicts one's current state of psychological energy is ready to work on consciously without crashing into mental illness. Dreams try to help the person function better by giving the truths that the person may be just ready to accept at that point in his or her life.

DREAM 40A: FORGET THE BAGGAGE AND LOVE THE KITTY

I was explaining to a boatload of people, which included my parents, how I swam from home to Tahiti. The home beaches I left behind were polluted and stagnant. The beaches I swam to in Tahiti were pristine and untouched by man.

As I was telling them this story, my old luggage kept getting in the way and tried to mix in and interfere with my new luggage. I then saw a sign written in German. The sign said, "The Energy of Sabrina Comes from Her Father."

DREAM 40A—INTERPRETATION

The "whole boatload of people" included many different parts of my psyche, including my father introject and my mother introject. My old luggage represented psychological conflicts, or "old baggage" from the past. I swam the ocean (emotionally navigated my way through my unconscious), which took me to a far and distant shore (graduate school was as foreign to me as Tahiti when I first started graduate school). My home shore was smudged and stagnant. The new shores of graduate school were new territory for my mind, body, and soul.

I am mostly of German descent, and I also took three years of German in high school, which explains why the sign was in German. My wife and I had a pet cat that lived to be eighteen years old. She died not too long before this dream. My wife noted that I was much more affectionate with this cat than with previous pets. Our cat was named Sabrina.

Sabrina was a real psychological presence in our home, as both my wife and I would talk to the other spouse by "talking" through the cat. This dream was congratulating and announcing to all the parts of my psyche that I had indeed arrived at new shores and could leave my old baggage from my family behind. It went on to spell out that the emotion/affection associated with the cat came from me, as I was her adoptive human father, if you will. The dream was also a condensation of the fact that I received more affection from my father than from my mother.

DREAM 40B: INCUBATING EMOTIONAL HEALTH

The author decided years ago to incubate a "big" dream. The first night I wrote the question "What can I do to live my best possible life?" three times to ingrain the question in my subconscious. I obtained the dream described below.

I was running a cancer screening center. No one wanted to lose their hair. The machine I used to screen patients was able to detect phonies. Every so often a phony was exposed by the machine. The female director of the clinic came out and said that I needed to carefully screen all the patients, so that we could refer all the phonies to psychotherapy. She insisted that was the only way they were going to put the cancer into remission.

DREAM 40B—INTERPRETATION

The dream was saying that to improve I needed to look at my sick parts. One criticism was that I was too concerned about physical appearances. The dream was screaming that I needed to attend psychotherapy for both my physical and mental health (I was screening for a physical disease, and the director was a more emotional part of my psyche, a female). I had this dream around 1991, after a multiple sclerosis (MS) attack. The dream screamed that I needed to be true to myself.

I went to physical therapy, took multitudes of supplements, followed the gluten-free MS diet strictly, went to Jungian psychotherapy, took the medicine and adjusted my spirituality. Around 2008, the MS started to go into remission. By around 2010, the MS was completely in remission, with no visible symptoms. I have some residual numbness and balance issues, which I am improving through physical therapy, going to the gym regularly, and taking the medication Tysabri—all of which is the subject of a future book.

Epilogue:
Research Tells Us
What We Always Suspected

It is gratifying that research is now increasingly support-ing therapists' and Jung's view of dreams. The view of dreams in the 2010 movie Inception agrees that each living thing, character, animal, animated force or celestial being is a projection created by our subconscious. As such, dreams often are relevant and have lessons to teach.

The PBS educational show Nova recently summarized the state of dream research (September 2012). There are five parts to the dream cycle. Sleep cycles through all five stages about once every ninety minutes. Four (4) is the deepest stage of sleep. REM sleep is the dream state and is the lightest stage of sleep. The sleep cycle goes from the deepest stage to the lightest stage about every ninety minutes so that it proceeds as 4, 3, 2, 1, REM. The cycle occurs five times if one sleeps seven and a half hours.

In the deeper stages of sleep (3 and 4), the brain reviews and refines memories of events that occurred during the day to maximize learning and memory. That is why one can often solve a difficult problem after sleeping. This has been known subconsciously by the human race for eons and points to the preference for "sleeping on it" regarding a difficult decision.

It was found that the lighter stages of sleep, which culminated in the REM (Rapid Eye Movement) stage of sleep, ultimately provide a kind of virtual reality, if you will, where the dreamer tests out new approaches suggested by the deeper stages of sleep. This whole process is important to the adaptability of the human race.

If a dreamer is awakened during the deeper stages of sleep (3 and 4), more positive responses are given on word association tests. If a dreamer is awakened during REM sleep, more negative word associations are given as responses by the awakened dreamer. It is thought that the associations are more negative in the dream state because of the evolution of the dream process.

The sleep cycle was used by ancestors to remember, learn and practice in the virtual reality dream state. This process evolved because it helped people survive. They mentally practiced ways of dealing with predators, which they subsequently used in waking consciousness.

During the REM dream stage, it is thought that the eyes are moving the way they would move if the dream were actually occurring. One loses muscle tone in the dream state because otherwise dreamers would physically act out what they were experiencing in the dream state. There have been people with brain injuries who attempt to act out their dreams while they are sleeping.

Dreams had a meaningful effect on modern life. When he was thirteen Albert Einstein had a dream, of which he remained cognizant, that forecast his Theory of Relativity ($E=mc2$). He dreamt that he was sledding down a hill faster and faster until he approached the speed of light. He noted that the stars and the scenery motion around him was fantastic.

A dream helped the chemist Kekule discern the structure of a benzene ring which was a major contribution to organic chemistry. The scientist pioneer Mendeleev fashioned the periodic table from the inspiration of a dream. The table he later constructed forecast the existence of three elements which were not discovered until fifteen years later.

Howe invented the sewing machine after dreaming of natives with spears, each of which had a hole through the spearhead. Modern research indicates that people are forty percent more creative after REM sleep. This writer had the frequent experience of finally solving a difficult mathematics problem after a good night's sleep.

MAKE LIFE YOUR DREAM

So this is the state of my soul journey so far. As a therapist, one comes to see that the subconscious is motivated to solve problems to gain further psychological and physical health. Going to therapy is difficult for many people because they are not yet ready to hear what their soul has to offer. People ignore the voice of the soul/higher self/subconscious at their own risk.

Good night. Unlock your personal power by listening to the guidance provided by coherent dreams.

If you enjoyed this book, please review it at amazon. com in customer reviews by following this link: http://www. drstevenfox.com

BIBLIOGRAPHY AND REFERENCES

Bernard, A. (2009). God Has No Edges, Dreams Have No Boundaries. Wheatmark: Tucson, AZ.

Bolen, J. (1989). Gods in Every Man: A New Psychology of Men's Lives and Loves. Harper & Row: New York, NY.

Bolen, J. (2004). Goddesses in Every Woman: Powerful Archetypes in Women's Lives. Harper Collins: New York, NY.

Bolen, J. (2007). Close to the Bone: Life Threatening Illness as a Soul Journey. Red Wheeler/Weiser: San Francisco, CA.

Campbell, J. (1988). The Power of Myth. Random House: New York, NY.

Chopra, D. (2000). Perfect Health: The Complete Mind/Body Guide, Revised and Updated. Three Rivers Press: New York, NY.

Delaney, G. (1998). All About Dreams: Everything You Need to Know About Why We Have Them, What They Mean, and How to Put Them to Work for You. Harper Collins: New York, NY.

Elsner, T. (2012). A Jungian Approach to Fairytales. Interviewed by Dr. David Van Nuys on Shrinkrapradio.com: Podcast #293.

Estes, C. (2003). The Beginner's Guide to Dream Interpretation. Random House: New York, NY.

Estes, C. (2004). Warming the Stone Child. Sounds True: Louisville, CO.

Fox, S., Sturm, C. and Walters, H. (1984). Perceptions of Therapist Disclosure of Previous Experience as a Client. Journal of Clinical Psychology, 40, 496-498.

Fox, S. and Walters, H. (1986). The Impact of General versus Specific Expert Testimony and Eyewitness Confidence upon Mock Juror Judgment. Law and Human Behavior, 10, 215-228.

Fox, S. and Wollersheim, J. (1984). The Effect of Treatment Rationale and Problem Severity upon Therapy Performance. Psychological Reports, 55, 207-214.

Freud, S. (1920). Dream Psychology: Psychoanalysis for Beginners. James A. McCann Company: New York, NY.

Hall, J. (1983). Jungian Dream Interpretation. Inner City Books: Toronto, Canada.

Hesse, H. (1922). Siddhartha. Source: http://www.gutenberg.org

Hillman, J. (1989). Blue Fire. Harper & Row: New York, NY.

Johnson, R. (1983). We: Understanding the Psychology of Romantic Love. Harper Collins: New York, NY.

Johnson, R. (1986). Inner Work. Harper Collins: New York, NY.

Johnson, R. (1989). He: Understanding Masculine Psychology. Harper & Row: New York, NY.

Johnson, R. (1989). She: Understanding Feminine Psychology. Harper & Row: New York, NY.

Johnson, R. (1991). Owning Your Own Shadow: Understanding the Dark Side of the Psyche. Harper Collins: New York, NY.

Jung, C. (1981). The Archetypes and the Collective Unconscious. Princeton University Press: Princeton, NJ.

Jung, C. (1989). Memories, Dreams, Reflections. Vintage Books Edition: New York, NY.

Masa, R. (2006). What Does Science Owe to Dreaming? And It's Not Pizza! Ezinearticles: http://ezinearticles.com/289366

Moore, R. and Gillette, D. (1990). King, Warrior, Magician, Lover: Rediscovering the Archetypes of the Mature Masculine. Harper Collins: New York, NY.

Myss, C. (2004). Sacred Contracts: Awakening Your Divine Potential. Hay House: Carlsbad, CA.

Myss, C. (2012). The Language of Archetypes: Discover the Forces that Shape Your Destiny. Sounds True: Louisville, CO.

Nova. (2012). What Are Dreams? Public Broadcasting System.

Sanford, J. (1978). Dreams and Healing: A Succinct and Lively Interpretation. Paulist Press: Mahwah, NJ.

Sanford, J. (1979). The Invisible Partners: How the Male and Female in Each of Us Affects Our Relationships. Paulist Press: Mahwah, NJ.

Sanford, J. (1989). Dreams: God's Forgotten Language. Harper Collins: New York, NY.

Taylor, J. (2009). The Wisdom of Your Dreams: Using Dreams to Tap into Your Unconscious and Transform Your Life. Penguin Group: New York, NY.

Watkins, J. (1982). We, the Divided Self. Irvington Publishers: New York, NY.

Woodman, Marion. (1990). Ravaged Bridegroom: Masculinity in Women. Inner City Books: Toronto, Canada.

Selective Glossary

Active imagination: A procedure to help the dreamer figure out puzzling elements in a dream. In a relaxed conscious state, the dreamer tries to re-dream the dream by remembering sequentially what happened in the dream. When the area of interest is reached in the remembering of the dream, the dreamer asks a character a question. The character will answer, given the limitations of the character and the situation. As in writing a fictional book, at some point, the book starts to almost write itself because there are only so many directions to go, given the situation already set up. This procedure, in this dream interpreter's work, seldom works because the conscious is still involved and often biases or distorts the answers obtained. The supplicant most frequently gets answers the questioner wants to hear rather than subconscious information the person needs to hear.

Anima: Jung thought of the Anima as emotions within a male. This writer believes that the term applies regardless of the dreamer's gender, i.e., a beautiful woman represents beautiful emotions within the dreamer, whether the dreamer is masculine or feminine. Animas are often classic beauties like the women in works of art by Rembrandt. Animas' appearance in dreams often has emotional healing implications.

Animus: Jung thought of the Animus as actions within a female. This writer believes that, as in the case of Anima, the concept of the Animus can be freed from gender limitations.

In this book, the Animus represents an action part of the psyche, whether the dreamer is a man or woman. Animus appears in dreams often as the **Heroic Masculine**, which has implications regarding the usually positive course of action being recommended by the dream.

Aphrodite Archetype: Named after the Greek goddess of love, female romantic and sexual feelings are represented by an extremely beautiful woman. Marilyn Monroe and Helen of Troy are examples.

Archetypes: Patterns of thought that are handed down through generations by culture and the quantum transmitting aspects of consciousness. Specific archetypes predominate with different people, so that one person has a collection of archetypes that define their personality (See Gods in Every Man and Goddesses in Every Woman by Jean Shinoda Bolen). Archetypes often form the different roles within society, such as mother, father, healer, professor, businessman, etc. There is special energy in each archetype that will propel an individual's life exponentially if the person ties into their dominant archetype.

Big dream: A dream of special significance that frequently reoccurs in the dreamer's life because the dream represents a fixated pattern of conflict that the dreamer needs to change. The reoccurring big dreams are usually identical with slight variations in the details or circumstances of the dream.

Chakra: In the Hindu tradition, chakras are center of prana, or vital life force energy. They are centrally located in the body and correspond to different organs and functions. The seven chakras include the tailbone, the genitals, the solar plexus, the heart, the throat, and the forehead, with the seventh chakra being transpersonal, as it is located above the head.

Condensation: The process by which dreams pack as much meaning as possible into each symbol. A symbol many times has three or four different meanings, all of them pertaining to some aspect of the dream. The multiple meanings can often have an ironic effect and/or have a surprising and insightful effect upon the dreamer.

Collective Unconscious: In Dr. Carl Jung's theory, each individual subconscious was connected to a collective unconscious, which was shared by humanity. For practical purposes, this ends up being the thought patterns transmitted through the ages by culture. This writer believes that the quantum transmitting aspects of consciousness are pervasive at a level we do not yet understand.

Course in Miracles: A course in which the student focuses on one of 365 thoughts each day for a year. The major point of this course is to impress upon the student that things in the world are not as they appear.

Divine Child Archetype: This archetype is often represented as a child, usually between the ages of two and ten, with ideal features for a given culture (usually blonde hair and blue eyes in Caucasian cultures, dark hair and brown eyes for Mexican cultures and so forth). The **Divine Child** represents the person's hopes and dreams for the future, i.e., "this is the child that will save us all." The appearance of the **Divine Child** in a dream usually involves issues of destiny and ultimate fulfillment.

Ego: The executive part of the mind that directs conscious decisions.

Heroic Masculine: An archetype of positive masculinity, it is the action part of the psyche whose motto is "To Serve and Protect." It is pervasive in main characters in movies, law enforcement, leaders, and the military. It is an action part of the psyche that literally is willing to die for those she loves or beliefs he holds.

Holding the tension of opposites: When making a decision, many people tend to make all- or-none decisions to reduce anxiety. If one decides one way or the other on an issue and holds to that stance, anxiety is reduced in the decision process because there is no uncertainty as to what one will do in that situation. The harder choice is usually a decision upon a course of action in the middle. There is tension because the person has to decide what mixture of the opposing elements to allow. There inevitably will be tension regarding following the middle road because one often will run into or unintentionally create paradox or contradiction. This concept is a strong call for moderation, which

Buddhists for centuries extolled as the better course of action.

Holy Grail: A chalice used by Jesus at the Last Supper. It was sought by the Knights of the Round Table in Arthurian legend because of its spiritual significance. Man's search for the Holy Grail is a metaphoric search for Soul.

Id: The part of the psyche ruled by animal instinct, i.e., sex and aggression.

Incubation: the process of asking oneself a question consciously before going to bed, which makes it more likely that a dream may emerge addressing issues related to the question. This book recommends writing the question three times in your own words right before going to bed to ingrain the question in the subconscious.

Integration: To be mentally healthy, all the different parts of the psyche have to work together harmoniously to produce one whole and coherent self, which is the result of integrating all the different aspects of oneself.

Interpersonal Level of Dream Interpretation: The dreamer's application of the dream interpretation to his or her daily life. The interpreter can describe the unconscious forces at the intrapsychic level, but the dreamer himself can best apply the dream to the proper portion of his social world. The intrapsychic level points out the forces and proclivities, while the interpersonal level of dream interpretation details how the scenarios seen in dreams are likely to play out in the dreamer's life.

Intrapsychic Level of Dream Interpretation: This is the first and usually the most beneficial level of dream interpretation. Every person, character, spirit, force, alien or animal in a dream is seen as a projection of part of the dreamer's psyche. At this level, it is all about the conflict within the person or how the various parts of the subconscious are likely to interact within the dreamer's life. Dreams are seen as a virtual reality play with a plot that makes sense to the subconscious, but which often appears as nonsense to the conscious.

Introject: Models of primary people taken into the subconscious which either guide and/or strongly affect the dreamer's day-to-day behavior and/or feelings. These models are of significant people, who each created a standard etched deeply in the dreamer's subconscious. When used as a verb, to introject is to make an image constructed from our subconscious perceptions of another person or persons, which is then used to guide feelings and behavior.

Lucid Dreams: Dreams where the dreamer realizes in the dream, while asleep, that he is dreaming and can direct the dream to do as he wishes, i.e., fly, super speed, x-ray vision, extraordinary hearing and so forth. Lucid dreams are the result of the conscious invading the subconscious and are of limited value because they tend to be simple dreams of desire.

Luminous: Giving off light and being singularly vivid in a dream because the symbol, scene, person or object has accumulated sacred, divine and/or transcendental (what Jung called numinous) meaning for the dreamer.

Multiple Sclerosis: An autoimmune disease where the immune system is mistakenly attacking the insulation (myelin) surrounding neurons. This causes variable symptoms, depending on which neurons in the brain, spinal cord and body are attacked.

Negative Mother Complex: Emotional conflict created by the part of a person's internalized mother introject usually primarily due to negative mistreatment by the maternal caretaker.

Numinous Experience: An experience which evokes simultaneous fascination, wonder and awe in the felt presence of the transcendent or sacred.

Overriding Voice: This type of declarative voice in the dreamer's mind is of special importance. The subconscious, in this case, gives up hope that the dreamer will respond to the meaning of the dream and delivers the message directly to the dreamer during sleep.

Out-of-body Experiences: During sleep, the person's vital essence leaves the body literally during sleep and travels through the world. This process is sometimes called astral projection. This writer believes in-body experiences are preferable.

Primordial: Symbols or conflicts buried deep in the subconscious that go back to the beginning of time or the origin of a person's life.

Post Traumatic Stress Disorder (PTSD): An anxiety disorder where the memory of a catastrophic and/or life-threatening event is riveted in the person's mind as if it occurred yesterday. Frequent recollection of the event and vivid dreams that are not symbolic, but merely replay the devastating event, are signs of the disorder.

Human-caused tragedies are usually more damaging to the person than naturally-caused disasters.

Projection: A psychological defense where causation for events is assigned to other persons outside of the self. Characters in dreams at the first and primary level of interpretation are projections of parts of the person's own psyche.

Quantum Physics: Branch of physics dealing with the infinitely smallest particles that make up the universe. These particles sometimes behave as particles and sometimes behave as an energy wave. They may blink in and out of existence, and their behavior is probabilistic rather than determined. The communication among the particles is instantaneous.

Queen: A very strong feminine or emotion-based archetype. The negative or **Shadow Queen** is most prevalent in dreams. It is domineering, ruthless, capricious, arbitrary and controlling. A good example is the Queen of Hearts in Alice in Wonderland. The positive **Queen** is seen less often in dreams because she creates no problems. Serene fortitude and perseverance to lead a family or country to greatness are hallmarks of the positive **Queen**. Catherine the Great and Queen Victoria are examples.

Recurrent Dreams: Dreams that deal with repetitive issues in the person's life cycles. The dream keeps offering a solution that worked well in the past or that the dreamer does not fully comprehend. In the latter case, the subconscious is repeating the solution because there may not be a better one available. Recurrent dreams virtually always deal with major issues in the person's life.

Savage Masculine: An archetype of male aggression or action to accomplish goals.

Shadow: An archetype focused on the survival and welfare of the person herself. It contains aggressive action, but there may be parts of the psyche in the shadow of which the person is simply unaware. For example, if the person decided not to become a minister, there is a minister in his **Shadow**. Psychotherapy frequently focuses on the **Shadow** as the most important element to change, i.e., the person either decides to divorce him- or herself from a part of the **Shadow** or decides to engage with a part of the **Shadow** that was not previously used.

Shadow in service to the ego: Using aggressive energy to accomplish prosocial goals, such as a soldier going into combat to protect his or her loved ones.

Sisyphus Archetype: In Greek mythology the gods punished a king by condemning him to the eternal repetition of rolling a boulder up a mountain, only to have the boulder fall back down the mountain right before he reached the top. This is an archetype of constant frustration.

Superego: The part of the mind concerned with matters of conscience, which may be prescribed by law or mandated by the rules and ethics of society.

Synchronicity: Meaningful coincidences. Things that are not related happen in such a way that they appear related. Synchronicity is often taken as a sign that a change in consciousness is proceeding.

Taekwondo: A Korean martial art that uses the principles of physics and focuses on the kick in self-defense.

Transference: A memory from the past similar to the present situation, so that the person's reaction to it is magnified and amplified exponentially.

Transformation: Complete and utter qualitative change.

Trickster: An archetype closely related to the **Shadow** that is the wheeler-dealer who, by his manipulations, makes an otherwise impossible situation functional.

Vision: A dream that feels real to the point that the person seen in the vision feels like an apparition in the real world to the dreamer.

Willing Sacrifice: An archetype of a person who gives herself as fodder or sacrifice for others.

Wise Old Man: An archetype that is usually an elderly man dispensing fatherly advice in the dreamer's best interest.

Wise Woman Archetype: An older woman who has special and almost mystical emotional knowledge such as a witch, crone, hag, or fairy godmother.

Zeus Archetype: In Greek mythology Zeus was the leader of the gods. Refers to the part of the psyche concerned with executive ego decision functions. The President of the United States, chief executive officer, or football quarterback are examples.

Made in the USA
San Bernardino, CA
05 March 2014